AMERICAN POLITICAL INSTITUTIONS

A Black Perspective

First Edition

David L. Horne
California State University—Northridge

cognella®
academic publishing

Bassim Hamadeh, CEO and Publisher
Michael Simpson, Vice President of Acquisitions
Jamie Giganti, Managing Editor
Jess Busch, Senior Graphic Designer
David Miano, Acquisitions Editor
Monika Dziamka, Project Editor
Natalie Lakosil, Licensing Manager

First published in the United States of America in 2015 by Cognella, Inc.

Printed in the United States of America

ISBN: 978-1-62661-289-1(pbk) / 978-1-62661-290-7 (br)

www.cognella.com   800-200-3908

Contents

Introduction

In this text, Black American (herein, "African American" and "Black American" are equivalent terms) politics is an exploration into the continuing attempts at achieving respected inclusion and participation by African Americans in the American political system, including their involvement in the establishment of that system. To understand Black American participation in the political system of the United States, students must simultaneously grasp the nature and operation of that political system. Black Americans were present when the House of Burgesses was established in Virginia, when the Mayflower Compact was agreed upon, when the Articles of Confederation were publicly debated and the first independent congress was established, when the British were militarily engaged, and so forth. Thus, Black American politics engages the political history of the United States.

Although segregation and separation became political terms that addressed Blacks "in" but not "of" the American political system, those were not terms accurately describing the origins and evolution of Black political involvement. This text attempts to provide a concise, comprehensive look at that involvement for the specific purpose of credible inclusion.

That involvement has been multi-layered and relentless. Even with the election of President Barack Obama, the Black American effort at respected involvement has continued unabated and challenged. As yet, African Americans have not overcome, since Black political success has to be more than individualized accomplishment.

Chapter One

Introduction to American Political Science

Clarity on the Concept: What Is Political Science?

Four Definitions

(a) Political Science is a social science discipline that is based on the use of the Scientific Method. The other social science disciplines are anthropology, economics, history, psychology, sociology, cultural geography, and urban studies and planning. The Scientific Method is a process for investigating the origins, establishment and development of any phenomenon—that is, any natural occurrence. The aim of the investigation is to discover, understand and comprehend the world around U.S. and our place in it. Western man tends to aim investigations at understanding phenomena so that the natural world around U.S. can be controlled. The Scientific Method includes five standard steps that are utilized worldwide, regardless of language, religion, government and other cultural values:

1. Hypothesis
2. Testing
3. Results/Conclusions
4. Corroboration (aka, Replication) and
5. Formulation of Theories (based on the accumulated pattern of evidence determined through steps 1–4).

The Social Scientific Method is exactly the same as the regular Scientific Method except that the SSM focuses exclusively on human behavior and interaction rather than on natural activities (as studied in Physics, Chemistry, Biology and the other "hard" sciences). This definition explains the science of Political Science.

(b) Political Science is also the process of studying who gets what, where, how, when, how much and who makes those determinations. It is the process of determining who determines the distribution of our social resources, from grades, to what clothes you have and wear, to what schools are available, to who gets a job and who doesn't, etc. Within that framework, everything in our world is part of a political process, since every part of our world is subject to judgments and choices about resources. Government is part of the study of politics, but clearly not the only part. However, in this text, government, as one dimension of politics, will be focused on.

(c) Political Science is the study of the game of politics—how it's played. There are only three participants in the game of politics—winners, losers, and those on the sidelines waiting to get in themselves. Those who don't learn the rules and procedures for winning are themselves played (they lose), while those who master the process constantly get benefits and their interests satisfied (they win). This text is about understanding enough of the game of politics to win at it—you are born into a political environment … and since you're in it, you might as well learn how to win it.

(d) American politics is essentially about competing interest groups, i.e., those who can best articulate, advocate and defend their common interests within this system in order to derive the benefits and rewards they seek. To be sure, individuals will most frequently make the crucial decisions within a political entity, but those decisions not only will impact groups differently—some will gain, while others lose—the decisions themselves will also be made in the name of, will be influenced by, will seek to help or restrain, interest groups. Such groups can be economic/political elites, ethnic/racial clusters, gender specific, sexual orientation, labor organizations, etc. They are interest groups to the extent that their members—volunteer or permanent—agree to coalesce around common wants or needs they intend to achieve from the political system and they are willing to actively struggle to accomplish those goals.

Each of us is a member of several interest groups simultaneously, but one or more will gain primacy in given situations. Thus, one may be female, African American, Californian, a college student, a mother, a wife, a daughter, a member of the working poor, a Republican, etc., in one American citizenship body, and either convince oneself or be convinced by others to focus one's attentions on important issues that affect any of those group interests at a particular time—e.g., as a college student, one may fight against tuition increases and as a female on a college campus, one may petition to have proper night lighting and increased campus security during evening classes.

The politics of competing interest groups, like all politics, are the dynamics of relationships, i.e., a who-who, who-what, what-what. Whether it is about absolute advantage, comparative advantage or compromise—the three principal political motivations—the issue at hand will always be about relationships. To understand the politics of any moment, one can focus the analysis on the relevant relationships at play (and the rules of engagement operating within that relationship). The political labels that apply—conservative, liberal, elite, family-oriented, Bible-belt, Black, Hispanic, White, feminist, etc.,—are always less important in understanding the political dynamics of a situation than are the relevant political relationships at play.

From the beginning of the relationship between a sizeable and significant Black population and an evolving English-dominated society in colonial America until the present, the nature of that relationship has been defined by the prevailing social value of the political status of the Black American population. Often that political status has been heavily influenced by the geography of the relationship, i.e., New England, or Mid-Atlantic, or Southern, and simultaneously the presence, extent and intensity of slavery and its consequences in those areas. But beyond those factors, the political status of Blacks in America has been a constant product of Black land ownership, Black legal rights and the opportunities to have those rights protected and respected, the political security available for Black Americans, and Black cultural authority. While the essence of Black political participation in America has most frequently been characterized as a struggle for inclusion, it has not been a struggle for inclusion in general. Rather, the struggle has been and is about specific inclusion—respected and valued inclusion—in the political-cultural decision-making within the residential areas in which Black Americans have lived.

A Summary Perspective of American Politics

American politics, like the politics in all countries, is essentially the conflict and resolution of competing interests for access to and/or control of finite resources available within our society. Interests dominate politics, and one either learns to identify, articulate, advocate, and defend one's individual—and more importantly one's group—interests, or one is continually exploited, deprived, neglected, disregarded, and/or disrespected within one's society. Politics is not fair, honorable, or biased towards "doing the right thing." Politics is what it is, a continuing competition within the prevailing status quo (the present arrangement of things) for greater access, leverage, and/or control. All politics is about attempts to acquire either *Absolute Advantage* (getting all of what is competed for), *Comparative Advantage* (accepting slightly less than all due to the relentlessness and credibility of the opposition to one taking it all), or *Compromise* (in which case each of the competing interests share partial victory, but no one gets all that he/she sought). The process of understanding, comprehending, and predicting interactions and outcomes of this constant seeking of interests and advantage is the study of American politics.

America has had two distinct and different constitutions. The first, the Articles of Confederation, ratified 1781–1783, grew out of the precedent experiences brought from England (English Bill of Rights, Protestant Reformation, common law, etc.) and the material circumstances of life under a rather loose colonial structure (single-proprietorship colonies, corporate/company colonies, and crown/royal colonies, each with its own rules of governance). After the War of Independence, this first constitution was superseded by the one we use now, the American Constitution, ratified in 1788–1789. The story of that evolution is fundamentally important in understanding what politics and democracy mean in America and how they both operate here.

In terms of its national and regional governments, America is a republican and constitutional democracy (a dual democracy). As such, America is a country founded on a legal document of some 10–12 pages, which lays out the fundamental principles, rights, restrictions, rules, and governmental processes for the citizens and residents of this country. Essentially, America is a nation based on the principles of constitutional law. It is also a country that is based on majority rule/popular consent and the regular election of representatives to handle the interests of a political constituency (republicanism). African Americans, Latinos/Hispanics, Native Americans, Asian Americans, and others who want to understand where they are in America and how they can influence a significant change in their status and their access to opportunities need to start with a definitive understanding of the evolution of the two American constitutions.

For all of its current complexities, layers, and confusions, government can essentially be divided into three major components that the constituency, i.e., the community, can influence: policy making, policy implementation, and policy personnel. This text and discussions will provide some clarification for all three.

Chapter Two

American Political Science: The Basics

B elow are groups of information that are considered critical to your development of a basic understanding of the operations of American government, and which provide a beginning insight into the operations of other governments in the world in which we live.

The Idea of Government

According to the most reliable data from archaeology and paleontology, mankind has been living in established social settings for at least the last 2 million years. Called the Homo erectus stage of development, among other things, this era produced rock paintings, innovative tools, and other examples of material life that clearly indicated the presence of human culture and society. *Society* here means the long-term habitation of two or more human beings together in essentially the same place and as part of the same group. An individual is not a society.

The concept requires human beings in the plural sense. *Culture*, on the other hand, means, among several definitions, that a group of people have produced enough things—language, clothing, eating habits, territorial residence, distinctive tools and/or weapons, hunting styles, housing patterns, social customs and rules, etc.—to distinguish that group from other groups. Culture is what defines us as specific groups with distinctive world views, ideas of right and wrong, good and bad, valuable and worthless, and the like.

Government—the concept of a part of any society being allowed to form and enforce rules and regulations to control the interactions of members of that society, to control the necessary resources to protect that society from attack, and to collect members of that society into a single body for public tasks—began, without calling it government, as soon as distinctive social/cultural groups were formed in the evolution of humankind.

Nascent government tended to be temporary and rudimentary (or very basic), but whenever people lived and survived together to hunt food and water, huddled together for shelter and for some form of body covering, and made war together to defend themselves or for offensive reasons, there had to be created a set of agreed-upon rules of order and conduct so that the tasks could get done. This regularly occurred from the Homo erectus-stage, approximately 2 million years ago, until the present. Government, by whatever name used during various times and wherever it occurred, has always had two basic purposes: *the providing of public services to a constituency, or members of a society,* and *the maintenance of public order and defense.* Whenever societies became incapable of achieving those two aims, the consequences generally included the death of that particular society or its absorption by a conquering one.

Government has also always been a cohesive force—a sort of glue—for keeping a particular society together as long as that government could perform its basic functions for that society. Virtually all early societies were *nomadic,* that is, the members daily chased their food supply, and when the animals representing that food supply moved, so did those societies that depended on that food supply. The first known organization of societies into self-contained groups was *the horde.* This was the population as a whole "united for common action for the common good."

Together this large group ("large" is relative here—the entire population of a nomadic society may have been 5 or 6 individuals, or, infrequently, as many as 100 or so) worked daily to solve the basic problems of all social living, any time and any place: *the regular acquisition of sufficient food (including water), clothing, and shelter for the survival of the members of that society.*

Out of the horde grew the basic individual family unit—male, female and child—and later clans, or extended families, and tribal groups, which were even more broadly extended families claiming some common ancestor. More importantly for our purpose here, what also evolved as a product of *the horde* was the first known form of real government, *the council of elders.*

This group, essentially a nascent oligarchy based on age and longevity, was made up of men (and sometimes women) who had lived and participated as members of a particular society for the longest times. Their collected wisdom and experience as hunters, warriors, protectors, etc., was deemed valuable enough to guide the rest of society through trials and challenges, and to make public decisions in the interest of the present and future of that society. The council, in turn, generally selected young warriors and hunters to defend the society and acquire sufficient food.

Eventually, these armed and relatively disciplined groups of warriors and hunters, in command of the weaponry of that society and familiar with swift physical action to handle problems, began to dominate the councils, which debated and meditated on public decisions. Out of this military dominance in decision-making came war lords and chiefs, and eventually a warrior chief called a king. While the council of elders maintained its importance throughout the history of forms of government as an advisory, deliberative and, frequently, as a legislative body, by the birth of civilization (approximately 3500 B.C.E.), as an evolution of cultural groupings into cities and permanent residences, the rulership of one or several military warrior kings became common as a relatively efficient form of government.

Other forms of early decision-making and basic government included *trial by combat* and *trial by ordeal or compurgation.* The former determined right from wrong, the best decisions, etc., by one-on-one duels to the death. The latter determined the truth or accuracy of choices, claims, and decisions by subjecting members of society to feats of torture and physical pain. Endurance of the pain was taken as representative of truth and accuracy.

Government as we have come to know it is a by-product of civilization. The latter process essentially involved a society's acceptance of systematic agriculture (which itself required fresh water rivers, effective and relatively efficient irrigation techniques, and tools for plowing, planting and harvesting), technological innovation, domestication of animals, a settled population, and writing to record data. From this combination of ingredients came the need to establish a regularized social order and delivery of social services, that is, government.

From the birth of civilization through the end of the last Crusade in Palestine (approximately 1343 C.E.), five fundamental forms of man-made government emerged from all the trials and error. Today, those same five are the basis of national governments worldwide. They are:

Autocracy—Rulership of a society by a single individual who is elected, selected, or who seizes authority through strong-arm tactics. Dictatorship is a form of autocracy.

Monarchy—Rulership of a society based on the family inheritance of the authority and credibility to be in charge. Frequently, kings, queens and other monarchs would claim "divine authority" to rule, that is,that God had selected them to be in charge and that they represented God as long as they were on the throne.

Oligarchy—Rulership by a small committee. The council of elders was such a group, as are various elites, secret societies, and juntas.

Theocracy—Rulership by a religious body that is at the same time a secular authority. Essentially, it is when the church and the state are the same, as in the early history of the Catholic Church, and later the Puritans during America's colonial period.

Democracy—Rulership determined by those who are to be ruled, or said another way, government determined by the governed. There is no single form of democracy, but rather at least five distinct types:

1. Parliamentary Democracy—Government dominated by a legislative body whose members have each been elected to represent the interests of particular territorial constituencies.
2. Constitutional Democracy—Government dominated by a written (or oral) document that establishes the primary rules and regulations for the entire society, and approved by that society through voting.

3. Republican Democracy—Government based on the regular election of representatives to handle the interests of the constituency that elects them.
4. Indirect Democracy—A broader form of acquiring proxy representatives that includes the election, selection, and appointment of such individuals to handle the interests of a constituency.
5. Direct Democracy—Government based on members of a constituency handling their own political interests straightforwardly instead of having someone else do it for them.

African Americans and American Colonial Government

The political-social relationship between Africans in America and the predominantly English American colonies began in 1619, with the landing of 20 Africans from the English ship, *White Lion*, which had seized the Africans from a Portuguese ship off Mexico. A second English ship, the *Treasurer*, arrived with 30 more Africans four days later. The Africans were landed at Port Comfort on the James River, near Jamestown, Virginia. The Africans were traded for food and supplies and designated into the Jamestown colony as indentured servants, not slaves. The indentureship meant 7 to 14 years of contract labor at the end of which, for the survivors, was the granting of land ownership, tobacco supplies, and status as a regular member of society. For men, this also meant voting rights in the local assemblies and town councils. In 1620, the first Virginia census counted 32 African residents, 15 males and 17 females. By 1650, Anthony Johnson and his wife, Mary, the former from that first group of African servants, owned 250 acres of land in Northampton County on the Virginia Eastern shore, and a few years later, two of their sons owned Virginia farmlands of 250 and 450 acres.

The legalization of slavery in Virginia and Maryland in the 1670s changed the status of some Black colonists, but not all. Black land owners retained the rights to file suits and testify in court, to expand their land ownership, to speak and vote at colonial assemblies, to join the Protestant Christian church, and to purchase contracts of servants and laborers.

During the colonial period, African Americans distinguished themselves fighting for the Patriot cause during the various insurrections against the British, and especially during the War of Independence, 1775–1783. They also participated in the French and Indian War during the 1750s. Participation in military service has been part and parcel of Black American belief in their American-ness and in increasing their credibility and status as Americans. Black Americans have essentially volunteered to fight in every war America has been involved in from its colonial days until the present, and as many heroes and sheroes as that participation has produced, interestingly enough, it has not had a major influence on Black American political respect and acceptance in society, from Crispus Attucks to Gen. Colin Powell.

Starting with Attucks, who led the group of outraged citizens on Boston's State Street against British soldiers acting as policemen during the Boston Massacre, and who had a statue erected in his honor in the Boston Commons as the first hero of the War of Independence, to Black Minutemen and members of North Carolina's Green Mountain Boys militia, Blacks fought alongside whites for American independence from Great Britain at Concord, Lexington, Bunker (Breed's) Hill, Valley Forge, Red Bank, Saratoga, Savannah, Princeton, Yorktown, and during virtually every other major engagement of the War. Names like Lemuel Haynes, Peter Salem, Pomp Blackman, Prince Black, Prince Whipple, Oliver Cromwell, Peter Salem, James Armistead, and others fought to gain freedom for America and respect for themselves. Over 5,000 Black American troops fought for American Independence, mostly free Blacks, but including thousands of armed slaves. At the battle of Rhode Island, for example, a rare all-Black unit had rescued hundreds of White Americans being besieged by Hessian mercenaries working for the British. In the fledgling American navy, Captain Mark Starling, the first Black American navy officer, made brilliant raids on British ships in American lakes and waters, sinking or disabling many British vessels. After the war, Starling's master re-claimed him and returned him to lifetime servitude in Virginia.

Finally, for this section, by the beginning of the 18th century, state legislation from New Hampshire to Georgia had created three classes of Black Americans: slaves, freed Blacks, and the free Black population who had never experienced slavery. Out of the latter two evolved the Black middle class that has advocated relentlessly for full Black American inclusion within America's political-social-economic life. During this period, this population included tavern owners, ship builders, sail makers, mathematicians, writers, blacksmiths, tanners, horse jockeys, wood craftsmen, and others.

Members of this Black middle class became the engineers and architects of the long Black political struggle for recognition of Black Americans as regular citizens, for protected equal citizenship rights, for cultural respect and for credibility in America. Even before the 1780s, when colonial America became independent America, Africans in America used a set of common strategies and tactics to pursue their agenda. These included (1) filing legal suits (2) in any way possible, attacking the existence and expansion of slavery, and its consequences, in America, (3) volunteering for armed military service in America's conflicts, (4) advocating (Usually with allies) for passage of beneficial state and, later, national legislation, (5) acquiring land ownership, (6) mass protests and petition drives, (7) political colored conventions and conferences, (8) pressing for educational progress, (9) gaining protected and exercisable voting rights, and finally (10) electing Black American representatives into local, state and national office. Before 1787, though these strategies and tactics would most often be pursued by individuals or by small groups, they would also be pursued in some simultaneous combination rather than in isolation, just as they would be in the following centuries. Beginning in 1787, and continuing to the present day, these strategies and tactics, formulated during the American colonial period, can be characterized as the primary *Black political process* for achieving full Black American political-economic participation in America.

Chapter Three

Precursors to American Government

There are several fundamental aspects of social-political interaction that highly influenced the formation, the type, and the success of American government, especially in its early stages. Those decision-makers who formed our first American governments brought much of this information with them as part of their own social-political education, they learned of it while in the colonial American arena, or they had access to the information in other ways. Essentially, distinctive precursors influenced the type, style, and substance of America's first governments. In this chapter we discuss ten of those precursors.

I. Nation-Statehood (Designation as a Country)

As stated previously, nation-state status was one of the consequences of the sixth and last Crusade (some scholars identify eight Crusades, but after the sixth, the Catholic Church was no longer directly involved), and the combined tribal groups of what would come to be called Europe. This latter term, from the Roman and Greek *Europa*, did not come into common usage to describe the continent of over 25 independent territories until the 15th and 16th centuries. More to the point, during the Crusades, particularly the last one, tribal groups like the Normans, the Saxons, the Franks, the Burgundians, and the Angles joined forces and surrendered their usual sovereign authority to a combined command in order to fight more effectively against the common enemy. This combination of tribal groups remained after the Crusades since it was recognized as a provider of more territory, authority, status, prestige and "power." This combination, by the middle of the 14th and 15th centuries, came to be called *sovereign nation-states* or *countries*, and its main ingredient was the concept of sovereignty (power over one's claimed territory, i.e., power to defend it, maintain it and possibly expand it).

The first recognized nation-states or sovereign countries were France (previously called Gaul, and various other tribal territorial names), Sweden, the Holy Roman Empire, Austria, Spain, and eventually England (a combination of Angles, Saxons, Normans, and Jutes). Within the feudal arrangements of authority that still dominated European territories at this time, the basic difference between a tribal chieftainship or private estate and early nation-statehood was that the former emphasized sovereignty as a private, personal control of land and the residents on that land. Nation-states required a broader leadership as a public trust, that is, the sovereign governed in the name of a larger group of people to whom he or she was obligated to protect and deliver services. Monarchies were the typical government of all of the early states, but they were inherited rulerships of a motley conglomeration of individuals and combined tribal groups who saw the monarch as a representative of the whole population, and not just as the selfish head of a private estate.

The Treaty of Westphalia signed in 1648 provided the first formal agreement and recognition among European territories of the criteria for being a nation-state. The treaty called for:

1. The principle of nation-state sovereignty and the fundamental right within territories of political self-determination.
2. The principle of legal equality between nation-states.
3. The principle of non-intervention by one nation-state into the internal affairs of another state (*principle of territorial integrity*).

Additionally, the Treaty of Westphalia called for international recognition by other nation-states to provide legal credibility to new nation-states, a defined physical boundary for each nation-state, and a defined population. Added later to the criteria for nation-statehood was if the territory had established a relatively effective mode of production for that population (i.e., an overall method of feeding and clothing one's constituency).

II. Imperialism

Imperialism is a derivative of emperor and empire. It is a concept applied to the physical conquest of territory by a more or less well-organized body of people who then impose their system of beliefs, their religion if they have one, their political system, and their economic orientation on the conquered group. Imperialism is a term of expansion and growth through the absorption of conquered people. Imperialism is distinct from attacking and sacking villages, towns, or other settlements, and then withdrawing back to one's home base. In imperialism, the conquered territory generally becomes a new part of one's home base, whether as a province, satellite, or new capital. Those defeated in battle, particularly the males, are typically either killed outright, made into slaves, and more generally over time, re-trained and indoctrinated to accept "citizenship" participation in the society created by the conquering group, most frequently as soldiers. Typically in imperialism, the females conquered are forced to accept new male authority and are utilized by the triumphant group to socialize the children of the conquered into becoming "citizens" and participants in the new order. Imperialism, a regular feature of early civilizations, is a primary process used in the growth and evolution of the Roman Empire from an initial small band of hunter-warriors.

III. Feudalism

From roughly 800 C.E. through the early 1500s, in the aftermath of the fall of the Roman Empire, the area now called Europe was predominantly organized by a political-economic system called feudalism. This system was also variously known as *the manorial process* or *the estate system*. Based on authority coming mainly from ownership of private property (especially land or real estate), feudalism involved societies in *relations of vassalage.* This meant that virtually the entire population in feudal societies lived in a hierarchical relationship of obligation and fealty either to someone or from someone, thus the saying "everybody is vassal to someone." For the purposes of this discussion, rather than to give a detailed elaboration of the complexities of feudalism, suffice it to say that residences were generally oriented around the land holdings of a landlord, with peasants, serfs, slaves, and indentured servants as laborers. The typical land relations were that the laborers would provide the man-power for the landlord's holdings (a castle, group of dwellings, etc.) including growing and storing crops, milling grain, operating and maintaining machinery, building and repairing structures, etc. In turn, the landlord was obligated to provide protection to his tenants, shelter, and order. The failure of either in carrying out their obligations was usually catastrophic for the estate. Peasants were generally itinerant owners of their own labor who worked through mutual agreement with the landlord; serfs were part of the land itself and were sold, traded, or otherwise moved when the land deed changed hands; and slaves were private property of the landlord. The other ingredient in this mixture was indentured servants, who were essentially contract laborers for seven or fourteen years, after which they were theoretically paid in coin or kind and free to operate on their own. Under feudalism, the Church owned lots of land, as did the local monarch, the nobles, priests, knights, and various other characters. The more land owned, typically, the more authority, prestige, and leverage one had.

IV. International Competition

Once accepted as a member of the nation-statehood fraternity, every country competed to be the best, most prestigious, richest, and most respected of the lot. International relations and foreign policies have generally been based on such rivalries, sometimes resulting in one of the innumerable wars described in most textbooks on Western Civilization (e.g., the Thirty Years War, War of the Roses, Hundred-Year War). This competition has typically been based on five major elements since before the Treaty of Westphalia, and definitively since then:

1. Mercantilism: This is a rivalry over how many ships a country could put into the ocean-going trade, and how much protection a country could provide for those ships. Nations with more ships had more

prestige and respect, and under mercantilism, ship designers and builders were the number one occupation. In more modern times, mercantilism has morphed into international capitalism with its focus on the amount of foreign reserves a nation has (dollars, pounds, yen, euros, etc.), advantageous terms of trade, and how much penetration a nation has for its products into how many other global markets.

2. Gold: This is a long-term and continuing rivalry over how much gold a nation-state has control over. Most of the world's gold supply has come from Africa (West and South) and gaining and maintaining access to those resources has been a constant point of European friction and competition. He who controls the most gold holds the might to enforce his will on others, it has been said.

3. Cash Flow: This is a rivalry over liquidity (cash assets) and the ability to move money over long distances. This has involved banking houses, financing of long-distance trading operations, insurance, etc. Typically, cash has been connected mainly to merchants and bankers, while those who owned real estate (land) and other private property eventually ended up selling out to that group or losing the property through foreclosure and default from loans on the property.

4. Import-Export: Every nation-state has to buy and sell, and import and export products, or else disappear as a country. This is a rivalry over how much trade and commerce a nation can involve itself into and profit from, particularly with a positive balance of trade and payments. This always involves tariffs, customs, taxes, and tonnage.

5. Political-Religious Authority: This has been a continuous rivalry over religious orientation and leadership, so that Catholic monarchs often massacred Protestants and Arians, and Protestant leaders in turn killed Catholics, Jews and others because as leaders they could do so.

6. Overseas Territory: This has been a rivalry about expanding a nation's territorial rights, its controlled markets and resource bases, and spheres of long-term influence. Nations with the most overseas territories, also called colonies, earned respect, status and leverage from other nation-states.

V. Colonialism

Colonialism has been designated the "most efficient form of imperialism." A central definition is the seizure or usurpation of property or territory already owned and occupied by an indigenous population; the establishment of a new social order in that territory so that all rights and privileges go to the colonizing forces, while the indigenous population retains none; the establishment of long-term control over the educational apparatus in that society so that current and future generations can be taught the "proper" relationship between colonizer and colonized; all for profit. The two principal categories of colonies are Settler (Permanent Occupation and Residency) and Administrative (Temporary).

VI. Commodity Production

Along with a number of other innovations learned from contact with Muslims during the Crusades, Europeans were informed of the benefits of landed plantation agriculture to produce crops specifically for sale in world markets. This process is called commodity production, as opposed to consumption production (growing food to eat directly, and only selling any surplus at the market). The laborers would typically be prisoner-of-war slaves who could be forced into labor-intensive, gang-grouped agricultural production in a disciplined plantation environment. The first such successful experiments in commodity production for Europeans were the islands of Genoa and Sicily in the Mediterranean, and sugar cane was the crop. This technique was then taken with the European explorers of the New World.

VII. Protestant Reformation

Once Emperor Constantine legalized Christianity as the state religion of Rome, in the 313 C.E. Edict of Milan, it became known as Roman Catholicism. The Church and the state were one, with Constantine declaring himself the head of the Church in 324 C.E. The evolution of Europe from that point on involved the growth, expansion, and politicization of the Church, as the official representative of Christianity, although Arianism (belief that JesU.S. was not divine or special, and that only God was divine) and other minor alternatives did have a parallel existence. In the early 1500s (1517–1536), John Calvin, Martin Luther, and Martin Zwingli, in different parts of Europe, started criticizing the Catholic Church openly, attacking the corruption of many Catholic priests, who, they said, were abusing their positions by profiting from dispensations (demanding payment for intervening with God for a particular client's salvation—the priests were selling salvation). Later, in 1530–1531, under King Henry VIII, the Pope was asked to allow Henry a divorce. According to King Henry, his current wife, Catherine of Aragon, could not bear him any male heirs to the throne, so she had to go. The Pope said no, that as the ruling monarch, Henry was the symbolic head of the Catholic Church and could not divorce—it was forbidden for Catholics. King Henry then abandoned the Catholic Church (at least in name) and through the English Parliament, created his own, called the Church of England, or the Anglican Church. This began state-sponsored Protestantism, or the growth of the Christian religion to protest the Catholic Church. Together with the initial criticisms by Calvin, Luther, and Zwingli, this was called the Protestant Reformation. Involved in virtually every succeeding European monarchy was the issue of Catholicism or Protestantism, that is, what kind of Christianity did one accept. Thus, under Queen Mary, a Catholic, the Protestants were persecuted, and during Queen Elizabeth's administration, the Catholics were killed. That went on and on. The Pilgrims, the Puritans (also known as Calvinists), the Episcopalians, Presbyterians, Methodists, Lutherans, Quakers, Baptists, COGIC, and virtually every other denomination of the Christian Church are all Protestants. Though some of the smaller branches still existed alongside, essentially the Christian world became divided and has continued divided into only two categories—Catholic Christians and Protestant Christians.

VIII. Social Contract Theory

Social contract theory, as explained and advocated in the 17th century, provided one of the main philosophical pillars of government. Essentially, it argued that a constituency, that is, a body of people, had to voluntarily agree to surrender some of their natural rights to be governed by a particular leader in order to get the protection and social order such a leader would provide. This voluntary agreement was called popular consent, and it was a direct contradiction to the absolutist rule of most monarchies. Sovereigns were to rule and make public policy decisions only with the consent of those governed—the leadership provided was given credibility and legitimacy only by that consent.

The two most widely known social contract theorists who influenced the formation of western governments were Thomas Hobbes (1651) and John Locke (1689). In Hobbes' view, expressed strongly in his book *Leviathan* (1651), before the appearance of unifying governments, man lived in an unfettered natural state with everyone having the license to do anything he or she wanted. In that state, man was selfish, immoral, and unsanitary. Thus, to Hobbes, before government, life for most people was "solitary, poor, nasty, brutish, and short." To improve one's chances of a better life situation, people must agree to be in a civil society and to cede authority to a sovereign leader. The people had to bind themselves to provide allegiance to that leader, and the sovereign had to provide protection and order for them. People were then expected to forgive the leader for mistakes and abuses of authority.

For Locke, as shown in his *Second Treatise on Civil Government* (1689) and *Civil Government*, it was a bit more complicated. Man's natural state, in which all were equal and independent, included reason and clear thought, and man had the natural rights to protect and defend his "life, liberty, health or possessions." However, since the world was a dangerous place, to live in groups and to better defend oneself required an agreement for a civil society to work out disputes, and a political contract with a sovereign leader to help protect the citizens and to assist in working out those disputes. However, if such a sovereign leader abused his authority, people had the right to remove him as leader.

Both Hobbes and Locke advocated a separation of powers concept for government with a standing legislature, elected by qualified voters, to make laws, and a chief executive to enforce and interpret those laws. In Hobbes' view, the legislative power had always to be secondary to that of the sovereign executive in whom power was always to be concentrated; to Locke, there had to be a balance of authority between them, or, more preferably, the legislative power had to dominate because it allowed broader participation. (By 1750, another political theorist, Charles Baron de Montesquieu, had added the necessity of an independent judiciary to the mix of the other two for a most effective government.)

IX. Citizens and Rights of Citizens

The concept and definition of citizenship has been a floating, dynamic perspective in that it has not only changed based on which city-state, territory, or country one referred to, but it also has transformed within the same territory several times. Essentially, the idea of citizenship predated Rome, but that territory is most often used as the model for the concept and definition.

Citizenship, at all levels, has required government, and it has meant a resident of a physical area who was born or legally naturalized in that territory. The citizen owed allegiance and loyalty to the government in that territory, and demonstrations of that loyalty sometimes required paying taxes and performing military service and/or public labor for government projects. Sometimes citizenship was a privileged status granted by the government and the social status quo, and sometimes citizenship has only been defined as a legal right granted by birth or due process. The essence, however, of citizenship through the ages, from Rome to the present, has been the presence or absence of citizenship rights and benefits. The real-life measurement, in other words, of whether someone was or was not a citizen had to do with whether they enjoyed specific rights allowed to other citizens in that territory, or even whether any citizens in the area enjoyed rights and benefits. Typical citizenship rights in Rome (where citizenship was actually a privilege, not a right) included: The right to vote in elections for civil and military office and the right to run for office (women could not vote and could not run); the right to make legal and binding contracts and the right to buy and own property; the right to testify in court and participate on juries; the right to sue in court and to appeal; the right to have a legal marriage in which you could bequeath property to your children; the right not to be tortured, whipped, or murdered, etc.

X. The Concept of Democratic Government

Well-read Europeans (and by no means was that the majority) were already generally aware of Athenian Greece democracy, with its Senate, elections, and restricted franchise. Most of them were also aware of the Roman improvement on the form called Republican, or third party proxy democracy. However, in the world of 16th, 17th and early 18th century governments, the most dominant model was still monarchy, closely followed by autocracy. Virtually the only European territories which even talked of participatory democracies were the Ukrainian Cossack military republics, operational in the 1500 and 1600s, an early form of republicanism in Switzerland, the Netherlands, and the early English Parliament, which was first elected in 1265. However, not only were all of these examples of restricted franchises, they were all complimentary to the ruling monarchy at the time which retained primary sovereign authority. Where there was any real participatory activity in Europe, it was most frequently at the town and village level where residents sometimes met in small numbers to elect a temporary leader, or the town as a whole met to decide on a response to a great challenge to the public welfare (an overwhelming rodent infestation, a devastating fire, etc.). Modern democracies as a dominant form of government, as far as European states and European emigrants were concerned, was essentially a 17th century phenomenon. Highly influential in that development was the 1688 *Glorious Revolution in England*, which saw a popular uprising overthrow the reigning king, and a year later, 1689, the Parliamentary enactment of the *English Bill of Rights*. The latter gave citizens the legal right to petition the government, to vote in Parliamentary elections, and a limited right to bear arms, all within a constitutional monarchy. By the late 18th and early 19th centuries, an elected Parliament (with a bicameral legislature) was the dominant English government.

XI. The Magna Carta and the Petition of Right

The *Magna Carta*, originally signed in 1215, means "Great Charter" and is the first significant written document from England that defines a limit on the absolutist powers of the king versus the people governed. Essentially, it is a document forced by the protest of nobles and barons (landed gentry or elites trying to defend their own privileges) against the monarch's non-recognition of any obligation to address subject concerns. On paper, the Magna Carta created the following rights in common law: due process of law, trial by jury of one's peers, and the writ of habeas corpus (appeal against unlawful and arbitrary imprisonment) by the king's soldiers.

In 1628, the *English Petition of Right* was issued by Parliament to King Charles as a demand to end abuses against the English people. It was a result of a longstanding feud—which saw seizures of private homes by troops to quarter themselves, arbitrary arrest and imprisonment for any-one who opposed the king, and heavy taxation of the population to pay for foreign policy choices—over authority between Parliament and the king. The Petition of Right represented a restatement of English civil liberties expected to be honored by the king, including: no levying of taxes without the consent of Parliament; no arrest and imprisonment of subjects (now citizens) without cause shown (reaffirmation of the right of habeas cor-pus); no quartering of soldiers imposed on the citizenry; and no martial law in time of peace.

XII. The Mayflower Compact

The journey of the Pilgrims (a sect of the new Church of England Protestants) from England, to Sweden, and eventually to Plymouth Rock, Massachusetts, forced a decision on them that they needed a different kind of leadership in this strange land. There was no Archbishop here, and no papal government to guide them, and they were generally opposed to the absolutist rule of divine right attached to kingship. So, on the Mayflower ship that brought them, the gathered group decided on a republican form of government for themselves; that is, the male Pilgrim church members would vote and make joint decisions on all matters that affected the wel-fare of the entire group. They wrote this agreement down and signed it, and it became the first written example of republican democracy in the colonies. We promise to "covenant and combine ourselves together into a civil Body Politick, for our better Ordering and Preservation," they said. It was, however, a restricted franchise. To be eligible to vote (you could participate in the discU.S.sion, but not the final decision), you could not be a female or an indentured servant.

A later colonial follow-up to the Mayflower Compact was created in Hartford, Springfield, Wethersfield, and Windsor, Connecticut, authorized by the Massachusetts General Court. A document was drawn up and approved in 1639 to establish the structure and powers of the combined township (Connecticut River Towns) government. That document was called the *Fundamental Orders of Connecticut* and is considered by many scholars to represent the first written constitution in the American colonies. The Fundamental Orders gave these territories self-rule, expanded voting rights to more men, and stated that all of the leadership in the colony would be elected by the constituents, not appointed by the crown.

XIII. House of Burgesses

In 1619, as part of the Virginia Company's colonial enterprise in North America, the first locally elected assembly of representatives was deemed the House of Burgesses (Gathering of Merchants). This was the first known example of home rule in the colonies and became the model for local colonial assemblies in virtually all of the colonies. Male residents of Jamestown who were considered of age (generally at least 21) and who met property ownership qualifications could vote for others to be a part of a legitimate group of public decision-makers, so that there would be uniform rules and social order to which they could adhere. The HB was patterned after the Lower House of the British Parliament and adapted to the rough conditions of colonial life.

XIV. The United Plantation Colonies of New England

This was the first formal governmental confederation in the colonies (also called the New England Confederation) and was formed out of necessity to protect themselves against hostile Native Americans (particularly after the recent colonial troubles with the Narragansetts and the Mohegans in the area), French incursions, and any Dutch privateers. It was a coalition of the Puritan harbor colonies of Massachusetts (Boston), Connecticut,

Plymouth, and New Haven, which was established in 1643 and lasted until the British crown reasserted its authority and revoked the Massachusetts land charter in 1684, and reorganized Massachusetts temporarily into the Dominion of New England. The coalition collapsed because of this assault on Massachusetts, its largest member. Rhode Island, which could have also been allowed membership because of its geography, was rejected as a part of the confederation. The group wrote and approved an "Articles of Confederation" agreement that provided for: a common treasury, an eight-person council of commissioners to resolve intra-group disputes and to vote on common denominator issues (each colony had two votes no matter the population size of the colony, and if consensus was not reached on any issue, a majority of 6 of 8 carried the vote), the rendition of runaway indentured servants and convicted criminals from one colony to another, etc. Essentially, the commissioners' council met at regularly scheduled times

> to hear, examine, weigh, and determine all affairs of our war, or peace, leagues, aids, charges, and numbers of men for war, division of spoils and whatsoever is gotten by conquest, receiving of more Confederates for Plantations into combination with any of the Confederates, and all things of like nature, which are the proper concomitants or consequents of such a Confederation for amity, offense, and defence: not intermeddling with the government of any of the Jurisdictions, which by the third article is preserved entirely to themselves ...

XV. The Iroquois Confederation and Constitution

According to the maintained oral tradition of the designated memory keepers of the Iroquois Confederacy, also called "The People of the Long House," and the Iroquois League, the origins of the combined national government of the Five Tribes—the Seneca, Mohawk, the Cayuga, the Oneida, and the Onondaga—was in 1451, based on the remembrance of the solar eclipse that year. A reconsideration of that date now has it at the year 1142, since that aligns with the historical solar eclipse in that vicinity. The two men whose names have been most linked to this foundation are Dekanawida, a Huron living among the Seneca, who worked out a treaty of alliance with Hiawatha, who was an Onondaga living among the Mohawk. After much discussion, this first alliance brought in the other three independent tribes and a verbal constitution was negotiated and agreed to by all of them. In 1722, the League was joined by the Tuscarora, and was known as the Six Tribes of the Iroquois. The Iroquois League began in the area of northern New York, but eventually expanded through both new alliances and physical conquest to control an area from southern Canada to Kentucky, and Eastern Pennsylvania to Ohio, a territory of over 1,000 square miles. Members of the League took different sides in the American War of Independence, with the Oneida and Tuscarora siding with the American colonists and the other four nations cooperating with Britain. This was a fatal mistake, and after virtually 750 years of existence, by 1784, the Iroquois League disbanded.

The constitution of the League, or The Great Binding as it was called, was unique among all other Native Americans. That agreement laid out operational principles and patterns for choosing, recalling, and replacing leaders, for conducting all joint business affairs, for declaring war, etc. It was based on mutual respect, unanimity of decision-making, due process, male and female voting, and the like. It was unprecedented on the American continent in its size and scope. In brief, here is how it worked: each tribal nation of the Iroquois League remained independent in all matters that involved their own sovereignty. The League created a Great Council of Sachems who were equal in rank and authority, and who were invested with supreme powers involving all matters pertaining to the League. Unanimity in public acts was essential to the Council of the Confederacy. In the General Council the sachems deliberated by tribal nation, which gave to each nation a veto over the others. Equality between the sexes had a strong adherence in the Confederacy and the women held real power, particularly the power to approve or veto declarations of war. The members of the Grand Council of Sachems were chosen by the clan mothers, and if any leader failed to comply with the wishes of the women and the Great Law of Peace (the constitution), he could be removed by the clan mothers. For every issue at the Grand Council, first the Mohawk and the Seneca Lords (council members) would have to unanimously agree on a course of action. They then sent their decisions to the Oneida and Cayuga Lords, who would also have to unanimously agree on each decision. If they didn't agree they would make a new choice and unanimously agree among themselves on it, then they would send it back to the Seneca and the Mohawk for their approval. The process would continue until both sets of tribal nations agreed on the issue or course of action. Once those four council members agreed, the decision would be sent to the Onondaga, the "Fire-Keepers." The Onondagas were the keepers of the meeting place and the sacred fire. If the Onondaga members agreed to the decision made by the previous four members, then that was it. If they refused to accept the decision of those other four, they could reformulate it, make a wholly new decision, or jU.S.t return it to the other four with their objections and ask for the decision to be reconsidered. Once consensus was reached the matter was decided.

XVI. Early Black Political Participation

Slavery eventually came to dominate the situation of being Black in America, but that was not the case from 1619 to 1669. Though there is only scant evidence available that a handful of Black men were baptized members of the colonial-era Anglican Church, and thus voting members among the Pilgrims and Puritans, with land ownership available for Black men coming out of indentureships in the colonies, there were other political participation opportunities available in town assemblies and local elections in most of the colonies. After slavery legalization became the norm in colonial America, free Blacks still enjoyed regular residential benefits throughout the colonial period, and Black men voted consistently in at least the northern colonies, including Massachusetts, New York, Rhode Island, and Pennsylvania.

In 1787, buoyed by the words in the Declaration of Independence that, "...We hold these truths to be self-evident, that all men are created equal, that they are endowed by their Creator with certain unalienable rights, and among these are Life, Liberty and the pursuit of Happiness," a few weeks before the constitutional convention, eight prominent Black men sat down in Philadelphia and agreed on a plan to create an organized collaborative approach towards changing the status of Blacks in America, and moving the race forward. These free Black men (some former slaves) included Richard Allen, Absalom Jones, Samuel Boston, Joseph Johnson,

Cato Freeman, Cesar Cranchell, James Potter, and William White. The organization they created was the Free African Society, which was a self-help, mutual-aid association specifically focused on providing burial services for Black citizens who were penniless and providing financial support to widows and orphans. The organization recognized the need to band free Black Americans together to fight for better, respectable treatment in America and to build and develop success stories among the Black population.

Out of the Free African Society (FAS) sprang the African Methodist Episcopal Church (AME), founded by Richard Allen, recognized as the first national organization of Black Americans. Also associated with the FAS was the series of Free African Schools established in Rhode Island, Pennsylvania, Massachusetts, and New York. In the latter, those schools represented the beginning of secular public education for all New York youth. The African Baptist Church, begun in the late 1770s in South Carolina, Georgia, and Virginia, joined this wave of Black collaborative activity, and through these associations, Black political leadership was developed (until the 21st century, virtually all Black political leadership came from training in the Black church), Black political strategy was formulated (petition drives, mass protests, legislative efforts, etc.), and Black Americans learned to work collectively for political effectiveness in America. The Free Colored Convention Movement was also an outgrowth of this activity. The distinctive characteristics of all these groups was the strong identification with an African heritage, the determination not to settle for discrimination, mob violence, and bigotry aimed at Blacks, and the resolve to organize to fight for self progress rather than to merely depend on finding White allies through whom they could fight for citizenship rights.

Through this early period of organizing, Paul Cuffe, the ship builder and owner, filed suit in Massachusetts in 1780 and petitioned the state legislature for being denied the ballot while still being expected to pay property taxes. He refused to pay as long as he could not vote, won his argument, and had his right to vote in Massachusetts restored. This case is regarded as the primary precedent for the Black American struggle for voting rights in America through to the 21st century.

Historical Document

PREAMBLE OF THE FREE AFRICAN SOCIETY

"Philadelphia, Pennsylvania

"12th, 4th mo., 1778—Whereas, Absalom Jones and Richard Allen, two men of the African race, who, for their religious life and conversation have obtained a good report among men, these persons, from a love to the people of their complexion whom they beheld with sorrow, because of their irreligious and uncivilized state, often communed together upon this painful and important subject in order to form some kind of religious society, but there being too few to be found under the like concern, and those who were, differed in their religious sentiments; with these circumstances they labored for some time, till it was proposed, after a serious communication of sentiments, that a society should be formed, without regard to religious tenets, provided, the persons lived an orderly and sober life, in order to support one another in sickness, and for the benefit of their widows and fatherless children."

ARTICLES.

"17th, 5th mo., 1787—We, the free Africans and their descendants, of the City of Philadelphia, in the State of Pennsylvania, or elsewhere, do unanimously agree, for the benefit of each other, to advance one shilling in silver Pennsylvania currency a month; and after one year's subscription from the date hereof, then to hand forth to the needy of this Society, if any should require, the sum of three shillings and nine pence per week of the said money: provided, this necessity is not brought on them by their own imprudence.

And it is further agreed, that no drunkard nor disorderly person be admitted as a member, and if any should prove disorderly after having been received, the said disorderly person shall be disjointed from U.S. if there is not an amendment, by being informed by two of the members, without having any of his subscription money returned.

And if any should neglect paying his monthly subscription for three months, and after having been informed of the same by two of the members, and no sufficient reason appearing for such neglect, if he do not pay the whole the next ensuing meeting, he shall be disjointed from U.S., by being informed by two of the members its an offender, without having any of his subscription money returned.

Also, if any person neglect meeting every month, for every omission he shall pay three pence, except in case or sickness or any other complaint that should require the assistance of the Society, then, and in such a case, he shall be exempt from the fines and subscription during the said sickness.

Also, we apprehend it to be just and reasonable, that the surviving widow of a deceased member should enjoy the benefit of this Society so long as she remains his widow, complying with the rules thereof, excepting the subscriptions.

And we apprehend it to be necessary, that the children of our deceased members be under the care of the Society, so far as to pay for the education of their children, if they cannot attend the free school; also to put them out apprentices to suitable trades or places, if required.

Also, that no member shall convene the Society together; but, it shall be the sole business of the committee, and that only on special occasions, and to dispose of the money in hand to the best advantage, for the useof the Society, after they are granted the liberty at a monthly meeting, and to transact all other business whatsoever, except that of Clerk and Treasurer.

And we unanimously agree to choose Joseph Clarke to be our Clerk and Treasurer; and whenever another should succeed him, it is always understood, that one of the people called Quakers, belonging to one of tile three monthly meetings in Philadelphia, is to be chosen to act as Clerk and 'Treasurer of this Useful Institution.

The following persons met, viz., Absalom Jones, Richard Allen, Samuel Boston, Joseph Johnson, Cato Freeman, Caesar Cranchell, and James Potter, also William White, whose early assistance and useful remarks we found truly profitable. This evening the articles were read, and after some beneficial remarks were made, they were agreed unto."

Chapter Four

America's Two Constitutions: Origins and Growth

The establishment of English permanent settlement in colonies in North America gained its first success in 1607 in Jamestown, which became the seaport capital of the Virginia colony. The expansion of British colonial territories on the eastern seaboard of North America (essentially, from the Atlantic Ocean to less than a hundred miles westwards) went from this Jamestown settlement through the 1733 establishment of the convict-populated Georgia colony.

Based loosely on the idea that colonies (overseas territorial acquisitions) were essentially of two major kinds, administrative (temporary) and settler (permanent), the British colonies in America were corporate chartered, single proprietorships, and direct crown colonies. Even the religiously based colonies fell into one of these categories, and after 1640–1645, with the exception of Rhode Island and Connecticut, the other eleven colonies were all made into royal or crown colonies. The practical effect of that was to impose a particular type of colonial government on each of the crown territories.

While the acquisition and sustainability of "home rule" and the maintenance of citizen rights was a primary concern of colonists throughout the 170 years of British authority in the area, the pattern of government established in the thirteen colonies was similar and (after 1620) included a bicameral legislature, an appointed governor, and a judicial council. The bicameral legislature included a locally elected assembly, or lower house, regularly called the *Colonial Assembly*, and the governor's appointed group of advisors, an upper house, which was regularly called the *Colonial Council*. This was a localized version of the British Parliament's elected House of Commons and the appointed House of Lords. In theory, both houses would have to agree on suggested legislation before sending it to the governor for approval and implementation. In practice, however, the governor and his representatives regularly tried to ignore the Colonial Assembly recommendations, and to use bribery and patronage influence to frequently attempt to control that branch of the legislature. The governor had the authority to appoint judges, sheriffs, militia officers, clerks, tax collectors, and magistrates, but it was the Colonial Assemblies that held responsibility for passing tax legislation.

The colonial governments through the years, particularly the Colonial Assembly, established the citizen expectation of rights of trial by jury, qualified right to vote for representatives, a say-so in tax increases, freedom of the press, right to own private property, and rights of habeas corpus. This latter was one of the common laws that came from England and were considered basic citizen rights in the colonies. Common law was judge-made law; that is, magistrates and justices in the field would make whatever common-sense rulings they thought fit the situation at hand, instead of following statutory laws on the books (even when there were relevant laws available, and often there were not). These common law rulings accumulated a body of legal precedent that other courts could rely on for decisions.

In the 1770s, in responding to increased colonial taxes imposed by Parliament (the Stamp Act, the Tea Act, etc.), and the British blockade and punishment of New England rebel activity, most of the colonies had created a network of communication and support called Committees of Correspondence, initially started by Samuel Adams. A joint committee decision to recommend the election of two delegates from each colony to be represented in Philadelphia at the first Continental Congress gathering was made and accomplished. This first Continental Congress, representing twelve colonial governments (Georgia did not send representatives), met in September 1774 to discuss common concerns and problems, criticized Parliament's tax schemes, and wrote a letter to the British monarch at the time, King George III. The letter asked for better treatment of the colonists as English citizens with rights, including the entitlement to be represented in England's Parliament. King George ignored the recommendations in the letter, sent British troops into Boston to seize weapons, and authorized them to fire on colonists if they resisted, leading to the firefight in Concord, Massachusetts. The soldiers were to continue all attempts to impose Parliament's will on the colonies. This hostile activity led to the Second Continental Congress, which first met in May–June 1775, and continued, with a winter recess, through the summer of 1776. All initial meetings of the Second Continental Congress were in what would be the first national capital, Philadelphia.

This Second Continental Congress (which was unicameral, rather than bicameral) declared the colonies independent from England and claimed nation-state status for the United States of America. France gave the new country the required international recognition.

Additionally, the Second Continental Congress passed the Richard Henry Lee Resolution in June of 1776, established the committee to write the Declaration of Independence (including Thomas Jefferson, Benjamin Franklin, and John Adams), and drafted the new nation's first constitution, later called the Articles of Confederation (see copy below) spurred by part of Henry Lee's proposal for a plan of confederation of states. Lee's Resolution called for the freedom, independence, and sovereignty of each former colony (and had been approved by Congress before July 4), and the plan of confederation was written by a committee of delegates and approved in November 1777. Ratification of these Articles of Confederation took four more years, and was dependent on the small states (Delaware, New Jersey, etc.) forcing the large states (New York, Virginia, etc.) to surrender the power to expand their land charters in the future, but it was finally implemented in March 1781. During wartime, many of the newly independent states altered their individual constitutions. So, by 1783, most of the states had a Bill of Rights with freedom of speech, assembly, press, religion; due process; right to face one's accuser; having a timely, public trial by a jury of one's peers; and rights to *habeas corpus* all contained within. All of the states still restricted the franchise, there was no universal suffrage in the new America, and all of the states recognized three branches of government—a legislature, a chief executive, and a judiciary. Virtually none of that, however, except the restricted franchise, was contained in the AOC, since to amend the AOC required all 13 states to accept any changes to the document. The two biggest influences on the substance and style of the AOC were the British Parliament, and the constitution of the Iroquois Confederation.

The Articles of Confederation established a "league of friendship" among the sovereign states, rather than a tightly organized national government. There was no executive branch or president, and no central judiciary. Congress was the sole national government and functioned not only as the primary legislative component; it was also the administrative arm. The AOC authorized Congress to establish five executive offices in order for the new government to operate:

A. Office of Foreign Affairs

B. Office of Finance

C. Office of the Navy

D. Office of War

E. Office of the Post Office

Powers of the U.S. Government Under the Articles of Confederation

1. To Declare War and to Negotiate Peace with Other Nations
2. To Conduct Foreign Policy with Other Nations
3. To Negotiate and Approve Treaties, Including with Native American Groups
4. To Borrow and Coin Money
5. To Equip the Navy
6. To Appoint Senior Officers of the Continental Army (which was really the individual state militias—there was no standing Continental Army)
7. To Coin National Currency and to Borrow Money for National Activities
8. To Seek (Request) Revenue from the States

9. To Invent New National Procedures to Conduct Business (e.g., creation of the ratification process requiring unanimity)
10. To Pass National Legislation (e.g., the Northwest Ordinance, which prohibited the expansion of slavery and set up an organized method of approving state applications.)

Description of the National Government Under the Articles of Confederation

1. Congress was an elected unicameral, not bicameral body
2. Each state had one vote, regardless of size, prestige or wealth
3. There was no national judiciary or system of connected courts
4. For regular business, Congress needed nine of thirteen votes to pass legislation and unanimity to pass amendments to the AOC
5. Congress needed a quorum of nine states to conduct national business
6. The states each retained their individual sovereignty and elected and paid their own delegates to Congress

Weaknesses of the AOC That Became Apparent After 1783 (Ending of the War)

1. There was no national government regulation of inter- or intra-state trade and commerce, and none with foreign nations
2. Government could not levy taxes to raise revenue
3. Even though the government could print and coin money, it had no resources to back the value of the currency
4. Congress had no real enforcement powers for its laws and stipulations
5. Congress could not effectively mediate boundary disputes between states or prevent states from annexing other territory
6. Government could not restrict exclusive conduct of business and foreign policy to itself
7. There was no strong, credible central government and no reputation as one—it could not preserve public order or effectively defend the country against foreign invasion
8. It could not compel its own states to comply with legally binding foreign treaties (e.g., the Treaty of Paris, which ended the war. States refused to pay debts to Great Britain and refused to either restore

property to Tories and other supporters of England in the war, or to reimburse them for their property loss.)

9. State courts could overturn national laws
10. It did not provide enough resources or access to them to provide an effective and efficient delivery of public services

Accomplishments of the U.S. Government Under the AOC

1. Declaring a constitutional, independent, and democratic government for the United States of America
2. Negotiating the Treaty of Paris peace document
3. The Passage of the 1785 Land Ordinance
4. The Passage of the Northwest Ordinance, 1787
5. Entering the U.S.A. into the family of nation-states
6. Writing and getting ratified America's first written constitution

Contributions to the Distinctive Style of American Governance Under the AOC

1. Unanimous Consensus as One Kind of Majority Rule in Government
2. The Ratification Process for Constitutions and Amendments
3. Giving Real Definition to Popular Consent and Popular Sovereignty
4. Allowing a Trial Run to See What Wouldn't Work as a Democratic Government in America
5. Bringing the Use of Political Leverage to an Established Place in Government (Small States Forced Major Compromise)

Black Americans and the Articles of Confederation

Except for, perhaps, John Hanson, the son of a Moorish father and White mother, as it has been reported, and a principal signatory of the original AOC, there has been little extant evidence of direct Black American involvement in either the Second Continental Congress or the committees that recommended the AOC. Mr. Hanson became head of the Continental Congress committee that had operational authority over government activity when the Continental Congress was not in session. Mr. Hanson was not, however, as some researchers have called him, the first President of the U.S. The AOC and the rules of the Continental Congress did not provide for such a chief executive office.

Slavery, as another big issue at the time, was not mentioned in the AOC one way or the other. Private property ownership, however, remained the primary value in the document, and states continued to regulate slavery.

Simultaneous with the summer "secret" meetings of the constitutional convention, however, the Continental Congress in July did pass the first major national government authority over slavery in the 1787 Northwest Ordinance (also called the Ordinance for the Government of the Territory of the United States, northwest of the Ohio River). The Northwest Ordinance:

A. Banned the expansion of slavery into any of the territories north of the Ohio River (which included the current states of Wisconsin, Ohio, Illinois, Michigan, and Indiana), although it did not free the slaves already residing in those territories.

B. Organized the territory claimed by the U.S. south of the Great Lakes, north of the Ohio River, and east of the Mississippi River.

C. Established national government authority to expand westward in order to create new states, rather than depending merely on expanding inside existing states.

D. Established the first geo-political border in the U.S. between the slave states and free states (the Ohio River).

E. Was re-confirmed in 1789 by the new Congress under the second U.S. Constitution, and was signed into law by George Washington in August 1789.

F. Created federal control of public domain lands and gave the U.S. government control of all unsettled land within its borders.

G. Created the first Fugitive Slave Law in the U.S. by making it a federal requirement for U.S. residents to return runaway slaves to their owners or to provide the necessary information to do so.

Historical Document

The Articles of Confederation

To all to whom these Presents shall come, we the undersigned Delegates of the States affixed to our Names send greeting.

The Articles of Confederation and perpetual Union between the states of New Hampshire, Massachusetts Bay, Rhode Island and Providence Plantations, Connecticut, New York, New Jersey, Pennsylvania, Delaware, Maryland, Virginia, North Carolina, South Carolina, and Georgia.

Article I
The Stile of this Confederacy shall be "The United States of America".

Article II
Each state retains its sovereignty, freedom, and independence, and every power, jurisdiction, and right, which is not by this Confederation expressly delegated to the United States, in Congress assembled

Article III
The said States hereby severally enter into a firm league of friendship with each other, for their common defense, the security of their liberties, and their mutual and general welfare, binding themselves to assist each other, against all force offered to, or attacks made upon them, or any of them, on account of religion, sovereignty, trade, or any other pretense whatever.

Article IV

The better to secure and perpetuate mutual friendship and intercourse among the people of the different States in this Union, the free inhabitants of each of these States, paupers, vagabonds, and fugitives from justice excepted, shall be entitled to all privileges and immunities of free citizens in the several States; and the people of each State shall free ingress and regress to and from any other State, and shall enjoy therein all the privileges of trade and commerce, subject to the same duties, impositions, and restrictions as the inhabitants thereof respectively, provided that such restrictions shall not extend so far as to prevent the removal of property imported into any State, to any other State, of which the owner is an inhabitant; provided also that no imposition, duties or restriction shall be laid by any State, on the property of the United States, or either of them.

If any person guilty of, or charged with, treason, felony, or other high misdemeanor in any State, shall flee from justice, and be found in any of the United States, he shall, upon demand of the Governor or executive power of the State from which he fled, be delivered up and removed to the State having jurisdiction of his offense.

Full faith and credit shall be given in each of these States to the records, acts, and judicial proceedings of the courts and magistrates of every other State.

Article V

For the most convenient management of the general interests of the United States, delegates shall be annually appointed in such manner as the legislatures of each State shall direct, to meet in Congress on the first Monday in November, in every year, with a power reserved to each State to recall its delegates, or any of them, at any time within the year, and to send others in their stead for the remainder of the year.

No State shall be represented in Congress by less than two, nor more than seven members; and no person shall be capable of being a delegate for more than three years in any term of six years; nor shall any person, being a delegate, be capable of holding any office under the United States, for which he, or another for his benefit, receives any salary, fees or emolument of any kind.

Each State shall maintain its own delegates in a meeting of the States, and while they act as members of the committee of the States.

In determining questions in the United States in Congress assembled, each State shall have one vote.

Freedom of speech and debate in Congress shall not be impeached or questioned in any court or place out of Congress, and the members of Congress shall be protected in their persons from arrests or imprisonments, during the time of their going to and from, and attendence on Congress, except for treason, felony, or breach of the peace.

Article VI

No State, without the consent of the United States in Congress assembled, shall send any embassy to, or receive any embassy from, or enter into any conference, agreement, alliance or treaty with any King, Prince or State; nor shall any person holding any office of profit or trust under the United States, or any of them, accept any present, emolument, office or title of any kind whatever from any King, Prince or foreign State; nor shall the United States in Congress assembled, or any of them, grant any title of nobility.

No two or more States shall enter into any treaty, confederation or alliance whatever between them, without the consent of the United States in Congress assembled, specifying accurately the purposes for which the same is to be entered into, and how long it shall continue.

No State shall lay any imposts or duties, which may interfere with any stipulations in treaties, entered into by the United States in Congress assembled, with any King, Prince or State, in pursuance of any treaties already proposed by Congress, to the courts of France and Spain.

No vessel of war shall be kept up in time of peace by any State, except such number only, as shall be deemed necessary by the United States in Congress assembled, for the defense of such State, or its trade; nor shall any body of forces be kept up by any State in time of peace, except such number only, as in the judgment of the United States in Congress assembled, shall be deemed requisite to garrison the forts necessary for the defense of such State; but every State shall always keep up a well-regulated and disciplined militia, sufficiently armed and accoutered, and shall provide and constantly have ready for use, in public stores, a due number of filed pieces and tents, and a proper quantity of arms, ammunition and camp equipage.

No State shall engage in any war without the consent of the United States in Congress assembled, unless such State be actually invaded by enemies, or shall have received certain advice of a resolution being formed by some nation of Indians to invade such State, and the danger is so imminent as not to admit of a delay till the United States in Congress assembled can be consulted; nor shall any State grant commissions to any ships or vessels of war, nor letters of marque or reprisal, except it be after a declaration of war by the United States in Congress assembled, and then only against the Kingdom or State and the subjects thereof, against which war has been so declared, and under such regulations as shall be established by the United States in Congress assembled, unless such State be infested by pirates, in which case vessels of war may be fitted out for that occasion, and kept so long as the danger shall continue, or until the United States in Congress assembled shall determine otherwise.

Article VII
When land forces are raised by any State for the common defense, all officers of or under the rank of colonel, shall be appointed by the legislature of each State respectively, by whom such forces shall be raised, or in such manner as such State shall direct, and all vacancies shall be filled up by the State which first made the appointment.

Article VIII

All charges of war, and all other expenses that shall be incurred for the common defense or general welfare, and allowed by the United States in Congress assembled, shall be defrayed out of a common treasury, which shall be supplied by the several States in proportion to the value of all land within each State, granted or surveyed for any person, as such land and the buildings and improvements thereon shall be estimated according to such mode as the United States in Congress assembled, shall from time to time direct and appoint.

The taxes for paying that proportion shall be laid and levied by the authority and direction of the legislatures of the several States within the time agreed upon by the United States in Congress assembled.

Article IX

The United States in Congress assembled, shall have the sole and exclusive right and power of determining on peace and war, except in the cases mentioned in the sixth article—of sending and receiving ambassadors—entering into treaties and alliances, provided that no treaty of commerce shall be made whereby the legislative power of the respective States shall be restrained from imposing such imposts and duties on foreigners, as their own people are subjected to, or from prohibiting the exportation or importation of any species of goods or commodities whatsoever—of establishing rules for deciding in all cases, what captures on land or water shall be legal, and in what manner prizes taken by land or naval forces in the service of the United States shall be divided or appropriated—of granting letters of marque and reprisal in times of peace—appointing courts for the trial of piracies and felonies commited on the high seas and establishing courts for receiving and determining finally appeals in all cases of captures, provided that no member of Congress shall be appointed a judge of any of the said courts.

The United States in Congress assembled shall also be the last resort on appeal in all disputes and differences now subsisting or that hereafter may arise between two or more States concerning boundary, jurisdiction or any other causes whatever; which authority shall always be exercised in the manner following. Whenever the legislative or executive authority or lawful agent of any State in controversy with another shall present a petition to Congress stating the matter in question and praying for a hearing, notice thereof shall be given by order of Congress to the legislative or executive authority of the other State in controversy, and a day assigned for the appearance of the parties by their lawful agents, who shall then be directed to appoint by joint consent, commissioners or judges to constitute a court for hearing and determining the matter in question: but if they cannot agree, Congress shall name three persons out of each of the United States, and from the list of such persons each party shall alternately strike out one, the petitioners beginning, until the number shall be reduced to thirteen; and from that number not less than seven, nor more than nine names as Congress shall direct, shall in the presence of Congress be drawn out by lot, and the persons whose names shall be so drawn or any five of them, shall be commissioners or judges, to hear and finally determine the controversy, so always as a major part of the judges who shall hear the cause shall agree in the determination: and if either party shall neglect to attend at the day appointed, without showing reasons, which Congress shall judge sufficient, or being present shall refuse to strike, the Congress shall proceed to nominate three persons out of each State, and the secretary of Congress shall strike in behalf of such party absent or refusing; and the judgment and sentence of the court to be appointed, in the manner before prescribed, shall be final and conclusive; and if any of the parties shall refuse to submit to the authority of such court, or to appear or defend their claim or cause, the court shall nevertheless proceed to pronounce sentence, or judgment, which shall in like manner be final and decisive, the judgment or sentence and other proceedings being in either case transmitted to Congress, and lodged among the acts of Congress for the security of the parties concerned: provided that every commissioner, before he sits in judgment, shall take an oath to be administered by one of the judges of the supreme or superior court of the State, where the cause shall be tried, 'well and truly to hear and determine the matter in question, according to the best of his judgment, without favor, affection or hope of reward': provided also, that no State shall be deprived of territory for the benefit of the United States.

All controversies concerning the private right of soil claimed under different grants of two or more States, whose jurisdictions as they may respect such lands, and the States which passed such grants are adjusted, the said grants or either of them being at the same time claimed to have originated antecedent to such settlement of jurisdiction, shall on the petition of either party to the Congress of the United States, be finally determined as near as may be in the same manner as is before prescribed for deciding disputes respecting territorial jurisdiction between different States.

The United States in Congress assembled shall also have the sole and exclusive right and power of regulating the alloy and value of coin struck by their own authority, or by that of the respective States—fixing the standards of weights and measures throughout the United States—regulating the trade and managing all affairs with the Indians, not members of any of the States, provided that the legislative right of any State within its own limits be not infringed or violated—establishing or regulating post offices from one State to another, throughout all the United States, and exacting such postage on the papers passing through the same as may be requisite to defray the expenses of the said office—appointing all officers of the land forces, in the service of the United States, excepting regimental officers—appointing all the officers of the naval forces, and commissioning all officers whatever in the service of the United States—making rules for the government and regulation of the said land and naval forces, and directing their operations.

The United States in Congress assembled shall have authority to appoint a committee, to sit in the recess of Congress, to be denominated 'A Committee of the States', and to consist of one delegate from each State; and to appoint such other committees and civil officers as may be necessary for managing the general affairs of the United States under their direction—to appoint one of their members to preside, provided that no person be allowed to serve in the office of president more than one year in any term of three years; to ascertain the necessary sums of money to be raised for the service of the United States, and to appropriate and apply the same for defraying the public expenses—to borrow money, or emit bills on the credit of the United States, transmitting every half-year to the respective States an account of the sums of money so borrowed or emitted—to build and equip a navy—to agree upon the number of land forces, and to make requisitions from each State for its quota, in proportion to the number of white inhabitants in such State; which requisition shall be binding, and thereupon the legislature of each State shall appoint the regimental officers, raise the men and cloath, arm and equip them in a solid-like manner, at the expense of the United States; and the officers and men so cloathed, armed and equipped shall march to the place appointed, and within the time agreed on by the United States in Congress assembled. But if the United States in Congress assembled shall, on consideration of circumstances judge proper that any State should not raise men, or should raise a smaller number of men than the quota thereof, such extra number shall be raised, officered, cloathed, armed and equipped in the same manner as the quota of each State, unless the legislature of such State shall judge that such extra number cannot be safely spread out in the same, in which case they shall raise, officer, cloath, arm and equip as many of such extra number as they judge can be safely spared. And the officers and men so cloathed, armed, and equipped, shall march to the place appointed, and within the time agreed on by the United States in Congress assembled.

The United States in Congress assembled shall never engage in a war, nor grant letters of marque or reprisal in time of peace, nor enter into any treaties or alliances, nor coin money, nor regulate the value thereof, nor ascertain the sums and expenses necessary for the defense and welfare of the United States, or any of them, nor emit bills, nor borrow money on the credit of the United States, nor appropriate money, nor agree upon the number of vessels of war, to be built or purchased, or the number of land or sea forces to be raised, nor appoint a commander in chief of the army or navy, unless nine States assent to the same: nor shall a question on any other point, except for adjourning from day to day be determined, unless by the votes of the majority of the United States in Congress assembled.

The Congress of the United States shall have power to adjourn to any time within the year, and to any place within the United States, so that no period of adjournment be for a longer duration than the space of six months, and shall publish the journal of their proceedings monthly, except such parts thereof relating to treaties, alliances or military operations, as in their judgment require secrecy; and the yeas and nays of the delegates of each State on any question shall be entered on the journal, when it is desired by any delegates of a State, or any of them, at his or their request shall be furnished with a transcript of the said journal, except such parts as are above excepted, to lay before the legislatures of the several States.

Article X

The Committee of the States, or any nine of them, shall be authorized to execute, in the recess of Congress, such of the powers of Congress as the United States in Congress assembled, by the consent of the nine States, shall from time to time think expedient to vest them with; provided that no power be delegated to the said Committee, for the exercise of which, by the Articles of Confederation, the voice of nine States in the Congress of the United States assembled be requisite.

Article XI

Canada acceding to this confederation, and adjoining in the measures of the United States, shall be admitted into, and entitled to all the advantages of this Union; but no other colony shall be admitted into the same, unless such admission be agreed to by nine States.

Article XII
All bills of credit emitted, monies borrowed, and debts contracted by, or under the authority of Congress, before the assembling
of the United States, in pursuance of the present confederation,
shall be deemed and considered as a charge against the United
States, for payment and satisfaction whereof the said United
States, and the public faith are hereby solemnly pled.

Article XIII
Every State shall abide by the determination of the United
States in Congress assembled, on all questions which by this
confederation are submitted to them. And the Articles of this
Confederation shall be inviolably observed by every State, and
the Union shall be perpetual; nor shall any alteration at any
time hereafter be made in any of them; unless such alteration be
agreed to in a Congress of the United States, and be afterwards
confirmed by the legislatures of every State.

And Whereas it hath pleased the Great Governor of the World
to incline the hearts of the legislatures we respectively represent
in Congress, to approve of, and to authorize U.S. to ratify the
said Articles of Confederation and perpetual Union. Know Ye
that we the undersigned delegates, by virtue of the power and
authority to U.S. given for that purpose, do by these presents, in
the name and in behalf of our respective constituents, fully and
entirely ratify and confirm each and every of the said Articles
of Confederation and perpetual Union, and all and singular
the matters and things therein contained: And we do further
solemnly plight and engage the faith of our respective constituents, that they shall abide by the determinations of the United
States in Congress assembled, on all questions, which by the
said Confederation are submitted to them. And that the Articles
thereof shall be inviolably observed by the States we respectively
represent, and that the Union shall be perpetual.
    In Witness whereof we have hereunto set our hands in
Congress. Done at Philadelphia in the State of Pennsylvania

the ninth day of July in the Year of our Lord One ThousA.nd Seven Hundred and Seventy-Eight, and in the Third Year of the independence of America.

Agreed to by Congress
15 November 1777

In force after ratification by Maryland, 1 March 1781. Signed by:

On the part and behalf of the State of New Hampshire:
Josiah Bartlett
John Wentworth Jr. August 8th 1778

On the part and behalf of The State of Massachusetts Bay:
John Hancock
Samuel Adams
Elbridge Gerry
Francis Dana
James Lovell
Samuel Holten
Paul Revere

On the part and behalf of the State of Rhode Island and Providence
Plantations:
William Ellery
Henry Marchant
John Collins

On the part and behalf of the State of Connecticut:
Roger Sherman
Samuel Huntington
Oliver Wolcott
Titus. Hosmer
Andrew Adams

On the Part and Behalf of the State of New York:
James Duane

Francis Lewis
William Duer
Gouverneur Morris

On the Part and in Behalf of the State of New Jersey, November 26, 1778.
John Witherspoon
Nathaniel Scudder

On the part and behalf of the State of Pennsylvania:
Robert Morris
Daniel Roberdeau
Jonathan Bayard Smith
William Clingan
Joseph Reed 22nd July 1778

On the part and behalf of the State of Delaware:
Thomas Mckean February 12, 1779
John Dickinson May 5th 1779
Nicholas Van Dyke

On the part and behalf of the State of Maryland:
John Hanson March 1 1781
Daniel Carroll

On the Part and Behalf of the State of Virginia:
Richard Henry Lee
John Banister
Thomas Adams
John Harvie
Francis Lightfoot Lee

On the part and Behalf of the State of NoCarolina:
John Penn July 21st 1778
Cornelius Harnett
John Williams

On the part and behalf of the State of South Carolina:
Henry Laurens
William Henry Drayton
John Mathews
Richard Hutson
Thomas Heyward Jr.

On the part and behalf of the State of Georgia:
John Walton 24th July 1778
Edward Telfair
Edward Langworthy

By the first few years after the Treaty of Paris was signed, it became clear that the U.S. government under the AOC was too weak to survive. Shay's Rebellion threatened popular uprisings and "mob rule" all over the new country, the British and French disregarded America's claim to sovereignty by openly abducting American sailors in American waters (Britain) and wantonly seizing trade goods and routes (French) whenever they wanted. Thus, at the Annapolis Convention called in 1786 by Virginia to discuss growing problems of interstate trade and commerce, the five states that attended the gathering (led by Alexander Hamilton and James Madison) took the opportunity to write a strong recommendation to all thirteen state legislatures to appoint two commissioners each to attend a meeting in May 1787 in Philadelphia for the purpose of making recommendations to the Continental Congress to amend the Articles of Confederation, based on the practical experiences they had all gained since the end of the war. Several states did just that, and in February 1787, under considerable pressure to do something positive, nine states of the Continental Congress agreed to sponsor a Constitutional Convention in May 1787, whose sole purpose would be to make recommendations to revise the AOC.

In May, every state but Rhode Island sent appointed commissioners to the gathering. There were 55 men in all, with an average age of forty-three, although most were in their twenties and thirties. Benjamin Franklin was eighty-three, and he was joined by at least seven other delegates who had signed the Articles of Confederation six years earlier. Seven delegates had been former governors of their states, thirty-three were practicing lawyers, eight were financiers and bankers, six were southern planters, three were physicians, and approximately half of the delegates were college graduates. At least forty-two of the fifty-five were current or former slave holders. This was not a gathering of poor folk, day laborers, peasants, or even small farmers. Instead, the Constitutional Convention was a gathering of men of means, property, wealth, and influence. The legal, private property, and merchant interests dominated the experiences of the men who wrote America's second and current U.S. Constitution. The Convention lasted four months, May through early September 1787.

To organize and manage the gathering, four quick decisions were agreed upon by the delegates: (a) General George Washington would chair the gathering; (b) All discussions and debates would be in secret—no public and no press; (c) The delegates would ignore the congressional restriction to revise and reform only the AOC, a new governmental document was what they were after; and (d) the Virginia Plan would be the basis of discussion for the gathering.

The Primary Interest Groups Competing for Dominance in the Convention

A. The Federalists and Anti-Federalists (Those advocating a new, strong central government to replace the weak, decentralized one under the AOC and those advocating continued strong state sovereignty and citizens' rights)

B. The territorially large, populous states (New York, Virginia, Pennsylvania, Massachusetts, North Carolina, etc.) and the small, under-populated states (New Jersey, Connecticut, Maryland, etc.)

C. Southern states (in which slavery dominated) and Northern states (in which slavery may or may not have existed at the time, but where it was it was not dominant)

The Important Compromises to Make the Constitution Work

1. Compromises on Representation in Congress

d. The Connecticut Plan combined the advocacies of the Virginia Plan, which stressed population as the primary determiner of the number of votes in Congress represented by each state (also called Proportionate Representation) and the each-state-has-an-equal-vote advocacy of the New Jersey Plan (called Equal Representation). Congress would become bicameral, and votes in the House of Representatives would be by Proportionate Representation or population, and the Senate would have two votes for every state regardless of size or population.

e. The Three Fifths Compromise for the Southern states, written into the first page of the Constitution, provided that five slaves were equivalent to three White residents for voting purposes.

2. Separation of Powers and a System of Checks and Balances Between Them (A tripartite system of government, following John Locke's and Rousseau's suggestions, including a legislative, executive, and judicial branch would be created with each being "equal in authority, but distinct in function." Each branch would have powers limited by the other branches.)

a. Ratification of the U.S. Constitution and all amendments would now be by a three fourths majority of the states instead of by a consensus majority.

b. Election of Congress would be by direct vote of the people, and the president would be both direct and indirect through the Electoral College system, as each state elected its own delegates based on its number of representatives in Congress, and those delegates would then cast ballots for the president. The state voters would indirectly choose the president by voting for the state delegates to the Electoral College.

c. Creation of a national court (the Supreme Court), but giving only Congress the authority to create a national court system.

d. On slavery, the delegates agreed not to abolish it, and not to require ending the Slave Trade into America until 1808 (although 10 states that attended the convention had already banned the slave trade, excluding Georgia and North and South Carolina).

e. On Civil Liberties and Civil Rights, the original Constitution is virtually silent. In the Convention, the Federalists agreed to provide amendments to the Constitution later, after it was ratified, which would guarantee citizens' rights. Those ten amendments, called the Bill of Rights, were added in 1791 (the Constitution was ratified in 1788).

Direct Changes from the AOC to the U.S. Constitution

Under the AOC, Government Could Not
1. Levy taxes on the public
2. Control or regulate state commerce
3. Stop states from coining money
4. Create independent president
5. Create national court system (III)
6. Amend AOC without unanimity

Under the Constitution It Could
1. Levy taxes (Article I, Sect. 8)
2. Regulate state commerce (I, 10)
3. Control coining of money (I,10)
4. Elect independent president (II)
5. Create national judiciary
6. Amend with three fourths majority of states

Regarding Black Americans and the U.S. Constitution, the group was poorly served by the document. The Three Fifths Compromise on the first page of the document (Article I, Section 2) defined slaves as less than whole persons, and not as men and women to eventually be respected as citizens. The decision not to ban the slave trade until a later date, as noted above, was included in the document, and the U.S. Constitution continued and strengthened the Fugitive Slave provision previously mentioned in the

Northwest Ordinance (See Article IV, Section 2). The latter was especially dangerous to even free Blacks, as more and more states, post-constitution, restricted the ability of Blacks to testify in court, even on their own behalf, and the provision allowed the wholesale kidnapping of Black residents and forcing them into slavery.

Chapter Five

Federalism and Other Methods of Organizing Government

Regarding the evolution of American government, the Mayflower Compact, House of Burgesses, the AOC, proportionate and equal representation, judicial review, and other such issues covered earlier, dealt essentially with the operations of American government, particularly at the national level. Clearly, there are other details about that operation to discuss, including the separation of powers, checks-and-balances, the interweaving of components of dual democracy, national elections, etc.

However, governmental operation is but one major category for looking at the American political system. The other major component, equally as important, is American federalism. It is the organization of American government between the national government and the states, and its evolution is the fabric of the political history of America.

What exactly does that mean? Internationally, there are three basic ways that the five standard forms of government in the world are organized: *federalism* (federalist), *confederalism* (confederalist), and *unitary* (unitarian). All three ways focus on the relationship between a central or national government and its district (states, satellites, provinces, etc.) government.

Under a unitary organization of government, the dominant financial and political authority is always located in the central government, and the relevant states or districts are dependent for their existence and operations on the generosity and political needs of the national government in power. This is sometimes called centralized organization, and with this organization public policy making is not shared, it is essentially controlled by the national government and imposed on the states/districts. Unitary systems are the most numerous in the modern world.

In confederalism, which is the opposite of unitary, the states or districts retain the dominant financial and political power, and the central government is dependent on relations with those states or districts for the resources and authority to operate. This is also generally called statism, or statist organization, and under it, any public policy decision made by the central government can be vetoed and changed by the states. Essentially, under this organization, the central government operates at the pleasure of the states/districts.

Federalism (or power sharing) involves a substantial partnership between the central government and the states/districts, with each of the partners having its own financial and political authority within the governmental system. For example, in the U.S.A., the national/central American government can pass laws, impose and collect taxes, spend public money and operate and maintain a national court system. But each of the 50 states also has the authority to do the same things at the state/district level, and even some cities (as local governments within the states) have home rule authority to pass ordinances, impose and collect taxes, spend public money and operate and maintain municipal courts. Under a federalist governmental organization, there is a division and a sharing of governmental authority usually based on a written constitution, as it is in the U.S.A. The legal foundation for both national and state authority in the U.S.A. is the U.S. Constitution, and neither the national government nor the state governments can dissolve the American system or amend the U.S. Constitution without the consent of the other. The states do not get their authority for self-rule from the national government and the national government does not get its authority to operate from the states. Federalism per se is not specifically mentioned in the U.S. Constitution, but what federalism means is laid out in the 10th Amendment.

Also of note is the fact that cities or local municipalities in the U.S.A., which often have their own authority as mentioned above, for day-to-day services to citizens (provision of water, electricity, public schools, police and fire protection, etc.) get that authority through state constitutions and don't have legal standing in the national constitution. States can essentially create or terminate cities, change their boundaries, grant or rescind local governmental power, etc. In effect, the relationship between American states and their local municipalities is a lower-level unitary organization.

Federalism as a governmental organization was invented in the U.S.A., although the concept had been written about and theorized for many years before 1788's ratification of the U.S. Constitution. Federalism is and was a continuing experiment, which is one of the reasons there are so many variations of it in American political history. In the U.S.A., federalism means intergovernmental relations between the three branches of the national government, the 50 states, and over 85,000 local, district, and county governments. Intergovernmental relations, which can be defined as the network of engagements between the national or federal government and all of the states with their local units of government, including conflicting laws and regulations and interstate compacts (or agreements), is a central concern for modern political scientists for public decision-makers.

Diagrams of Three Types of Governmental Organization

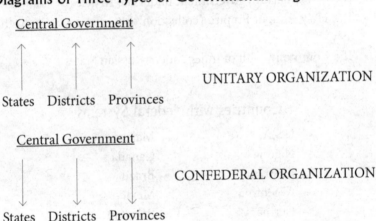

Central Government

UNITARY ORGANIZATION

States   Districts   Provinces

Central Government

CONFEDERAL ORGANIZATION

States   Districts   Provinces

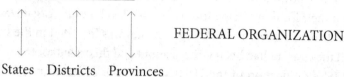

Central Government

FEDERAL ORGANIZATION

States   Districts   Provinces

Countries with Unitary Systems (Over 75% of the World)

England	Belgium	Bulgaria	Italy
France	The Netherlands	Japan	Sweden
Israel	Poland	Spain	

Countries with Confederal Systems

- The European Union (EU) (15 European countries)
- The United States of the Confederacy (during the Civil War)
- The first American government under the Articles of Confederation
- The Holy Roman Empire (collection of German states—16th century)
- The Commonwealth of Independent Russian States

Countries with Federal Systems

U.S.A.	Malaysia
Nigeria	Canada
Australia	Brazil
Argentina	Mexico
Germany	Pakistan
India	United Arab Emirates
Switzerland	Venezuela

The U.S. Constitution and Federalism

(Identifying Powers to National or State Government)

- Delegated or Enumerated Powers (National—Articles I, II, III, V)
- Express Powers (National—Article I, Section 8)
- Implied Powers (National—Necessary and Proper Clause)
- Reserved Powers (States—Amendment 10)
- Concurrent Powers (Powers simultaneously authorized to National and State governments, such as taxes, education, police, criminal and property law, social welfare, etc.—Articles I, IV, V)
- Inherent Powers (National government powers inherited by being a country, such as appointing ambassadors, going to war, treaties, international debts—Article I, Section 8)

Different Types of Federalism over the Years

Most U.S. presidents have had their own adaptation to federalism.

1. State-Centered Federalism, 1787–1868: The states were expected to solve American public policy problems more than the national government until after the Civil War.
2. Dual Federalism, 1868–1913: Also called Layer Cake or Horizontal
3. Federalism: this type depended on the national government focusing on its specific foreign policy duties while the states took care of most domestic issues in the country. Like a layer cake, federal duties were separated from state duties.
4. Cooperative Federalism, 1913–1964: Also called Marble Cake Federalism, this type involved extensive intertwining of responsibilities, and a shift towards stronger national intervention (e.g., the Depression, two World Worlds, the birth of the Federal Income Tax). Thus, both the national and state governments handled public assistance, welfare, public housing, urban renovation, etc., while the national government intervened in labor disputes, massive public works projects, business practices, etc. Like a marble cake, the duties were no longer separate and distinct.

5. Centralized Federalism, 1964–1980: Also called Pineapple Upside-Down Cake Federalism, since the national government essentially ignored the viewpoint that the states had their own territoriality in terms of issues and programs—the "icing moving to the top," so to speak. Thus, Great Society Programs (Lyndon Johnson) and Enterprise Zones (Richard Nixon) and other federal projects intervened into virtually all problems confronting the American public, from air pollution and toxic waste dumps, to home insulation, noise reduction, water district problems, street beautification, and consumer safety. The states were deemed incapable of handling much of anything during this time, including who could drink alcohol and who could smoke cigarettes.

6. New Federalism, 1980–1985: Also called States' Rights Federalism, and while it was introduced by President Nixon, it was popularized by President Reagan. It was a grand attempt at reducing the dominance of the federal government in handling domestic issues and giving that responsibility back to the states. This meant less money to the states and more expectations of state self-reliance.

7. Representational Federalism, 1985–the present: Also called Election Federalism, since this era is based on the Supreme Court's ruling in *Garcia v. San Antonio Metropolitan Transit*, that the only constitutional protection the states had in terms of avoiding federal involvement in their affairs was the states' handling of elections to Congress and to the presidency. All else was within the federal domain.

Important Historical Decisions in the Evolution of American Federalism

These are deemed the most significant milestones in what federalism means and how it works in America:

1. The Supreme Court's decision in *McCulloch v. Maryland*, 1819, that not only gave the Court the power to interpret the U.S. Constitution, but regarding federalism, the Court said that through the Elastic Clause, otherwise known as the "Necessary and Proper Clause" in Article I, and the Supremacy Clause in Article VI, in a conflict of

authority between the national government and the states, the federal law was supreme.

2. The defeat of the South in the American Civil War, thus nullifying state sovereignty, for all intents and purposes.

3. The 14th Amendment to the U.S. Constitution, which allowed what is called a national civil rights system (using the 14th Amendment's due process or equal protection clauses invoked most of the rest of the relevant ten amendments).

4. The expansion of federal authority over state trading regulations through the Interstate Commerce Clause of the Constitution.

5. The 16th Amendment's creation of the Federal Income Tax, which allowed for the growth of enormous federal revenue to either assist the states or withhold from the states.

6. The Supreme Court's ruling in *Garcia v. San Antonio Metro*, 1985.

Federal Control of the Federalist Partnership

Even though federalism, *de jure*, is a partnership based on the sharing of powers between the national government and the state governments, essentially the national or federal government is the more equal partner in this relationship, *de facto*. That is because of the six historical items above, and also because of the components of federal control continually used in the relationship. Those components are:

A. Money

(1) *Federal grants-in-aid* to the states, which are usually for a specific purpose and quite often require matching funds. These are the most numerous of financial provisions from the national to the state government and allow federal control of much of the state budgets, since these grants are in virtually every category of state and local government activity.

    a. *Categorical Funds*, which are always for a specific purpose (like Pell Grant funds, which can only be used for students). These are funds with strings attached, and are not favored by states.

    b. *Block Grants*, which allow states to spend in major areas of need, such as state health services, drug abuse clinics, and mental health services, community development. Block grants allow states far more freedom to choose how to spend the funds, and are thus heavily favored by the states.

(2) *General Purpose Grants* allow states to choose virtually without restriction where they will spend the funds, and they can usually be provided without a matching requirement. Thus, these types of grants are the most popular with the states, but are the least likely to be granted by the federal government.

B. Pre-emption

(1) *Total pre-emption* means that the national government imposes its authority in an area that is traditionally handled by the state, and prohibits the state from handling the issue as long as the federal government remains interested in it. Such areas are copyright protection, regulation of railroads and banking, and bankruptcy stipulations.

(2) *Partial pre-emption* means the national government will allow the state standard to operate in an area as long as the state law does not conflict with federal law, but will also carefully monitor, or look over the shoulder of, state regulators to ensure they are complying with federal guidelines on the issue.

(3) *Unfunded Mandates.* These occur when the federal government orders the state to perform some public service activity without providing any funding for it, and virtually forcing the state to comply. One recent example of this was the federal government's order to the L.A. County Supervisors to immediately purchase 700 new buses for L.A. riders and to use some of the federal transportation money it had already provided to the state and county. Failure to comply would mean reducing or terminating the following year's allocation of funding. After much political maneuvering, L.A. finally got the new buses.

African Americans and Federalism in America

The single most significant political mechanism within the American political system, as it pertains to African Americans, is federalism. Overall, though there have been significant positive gains, federalism has been a governmental process through which African Americans have had their opportunities for political participation undermined and stunted through states' rights. In general, as the national government centralized more authority within the national/states partnership, the increased participation of African Americans was (has been) a result. As stated by one political scientist, "For African Americans, federalism may have had more to do with destroying (political) freedom than with encouraging it. The main beneficiaries of federalism throughout American political history have been southern Whites, who have been given the freedom (through state sovereignty) to oppress Negroes first as slaves and later as a depressed caste."

On the positive side, African Americans used federalism to escape slavery into non-slave states (slavery laws until the 19th century, were virtually all state laws, not federal). From the 1920s to the 1950s, African Americans used federalism as a basis for the Great Migration of Blacks out of the South and into the North and Northwest. In the 20th century, Blacks also used federalism to help achieve the ballot and elective offices in local and state elections.

Historically, federalism has been used to maintain slavery in America; to construct and perpetuate Jim Crowism; to allow states to ban free Black Americans; to depress Black voting rights and political participation; to block the enactment of beneficial educational and welfare legislation such as the Blair Education Bill and the Elementary and Secondary Education Act; and to protect lynching and other forms of violence against Black Americans.

The waxing and waning of states rights leverage versus "big government" federal authority, as advocated by one presidential administration or the other, has been the engine of the political roller coaster of Black political involvement in America.

Chapter Six

Organization and Comments on the U.S. Constitution

Organization of the Constitution

The original U.S. Constitution (shown below) is an approximately 4,543-word document arranged into 7 principal articles, with the first four articles having an average of five sections each (Article I has 10 sections, while the other three each contain three or four sections apiece, a grand total of 21 sections). Article I lays out the qualifications of U.S. Congress persons, the power, range and authority of Congress, and also (since Congress was indeed our first national government) in Article I, Section 8, the express powers of the federal government in general. Article II does the same for the presidency, and Article III identifies the federal court.

Article IV is about the full faith and credit states are to give to each other's laws, including honoring all established privileges and immunities of citizens, the acceptance process for territories to become states within the United States, the definition of extradition and rendition, and the national government's promise to provide a republican form of leadership selection to the states and to protect the states from both external invasion and domestic violence.

Article V describes the proposal and ratification of amendments to the Constitution, and how to call a constitutional convention (there's been only one in American history). Article VI describes the supremacy of the national government in relationships between the central government and the states, obligates the national government to pay its legal debts, and establishes the need for all nationally elected officials to be bound by an oath or affirmation to support the American Constitution. Article VII merely establishes the three fourths majority needed to ratify the U.S. Constitution. It should be noted that there are no specifically written sections in Articles V, VI, and VII.

Tripartite Authority Provided in the Constitution

Again, *de jure*, the theory is that each major branch of the U.S.A. federal government is equal in authority but different and distinct in function. However, even on the surface of things, that did not seem to be reality. Article I takes up approximately two and a half pages of the Constitution; Article II, one and a half pages; and Article III, a mere half page.

The Constitution provides several types of authority to the different branches of government.

A.   Inherent Powers, which are those not directly stated in the Constitution, but which come with being a nation-state or country that is internationally recognized within the family of nations. Thus, the national government of the U.S.A. began officially operating with the declaration of the "United Colonies of America" by the Second Continental Congress in June, 1776, and the recognition of that government by the French. However, the government of the U.S.A. did not become legally binding unto itself and to the rest of the world until the ratification of the Articles of Confederation in 1781. That government "inherited" the power that other countries had to appoint ambassadors, declare and conduct war, make binding treaties, assume and pay international debts, etc. (See Article 1, Section 8)

B.   Express Powers, which are those principles of national legislative and administrative authority provided to the central government in general, for example, to establish a post office, to establish a national military, and to coin national currency. (See Article I, Section 8)

C.   Delegated or Enumerated Powers, which are the specific range and scope of authority provided to each branch of the national government. For example, only Congress can declare war, the president is the commander-in-chief, and the Court handles legal disputes between states. (See Articles I, II, III, and V)

D.   Implied Powers, which are elements of authority provided to Congress by the "Necessary and Proper Clause" in the Constitution, as interpreted by the federal courts, to "make whatever laws Congress deems necessary and proper" for the United States (See Article I, Section 8)

E.   Concurrent Powers, which are parallel elements of authority by both the national government and the states over the same general area of public need, but through different approaches, e.g., taxes, education, elections, police, criminal and property law, and social welfare. (See Articles I, IV, V)

F.   Reserve Power, which is the retention by the states of all public authority not specifically designated in the Constitution to the central government, and not specifically denied to the states by the U.S. Constitution. This power was not in the original Constitution ratified in 1788, but was added in 1791 with the first ten amendments. (See Amendment 10)

Important Constitutional Clauses (*Phrases and sections of the constitution that have been interpreted by the federal courts as important principles and reference point markers within the document)

In the Original U.S. Constitution

A.   Supremacy Clause (Art. VI)
B.   Necessary and Proper Clause (aka, the Elastic Clause) (Art. I)
C.   Full Faith and Credit Clause (Art. V)
D.   Privileges and Immunities Clause (Art. V)
E.   Commerce Clause (Art. I)

Added by Amendments to the U.S. Constitution

A. Establishment Clause (Amend. I)
B. Due Process Clause (Amend. V)
C. Reserve Clause (Amend. X)
D. Rights Retention Clause (Amend. IX)

Historical Document

The Constitution for the United States of America

We the People of the United States, in Order to form a more perfect Union, establish Justice, insure domestic Tranquility, provide for the common defence, promote the general Welfare, and secure the Blessings of Liberty to ourselves and our Posterity, do ordain and establish this Constitution for the United States of America.

Article. I.

Section. 1. All legislative Powers herein granted shall be vested in a Congress of the United States, which shall consist of a Senate and House of Representatives.

Section. 2. The House of Representatives shall be composed of Members chosen every second Year by the People of the several States, and the Electors in each State shall have the Qualifications requisite for Electors of the most numerous Branch of the State Legislature.

No Person shall be a Representative who shall not have attained to the Age of twenty five Years, and been seven Years a Citizen of the United States, and who shall not, when elected, be an Inhabitant of that State in which he shall be chosen.

Representatives and direct Taxes shall be apportioned among the several States which may be included within this Union, according to their respective Numbers, which shall be determined by adding to the whole Number of free Persons, including those bound to Service for a Term of Years, and excluding Indians not taxed, *three fifths of all other Persons.* The actual Enumeration shall be made within three Years after the first Meeting of the Congress of the United States, and within every subsequent Term of ten Years, in such Manner as they shall by Law direct. The Number of Representatives shall not exceed one for every thirty ThousA. nd, but each State shall have at Least one Representative; and until such enumeration shall be made, the State of New Hampshire shall be entitled to chuse three, Massachusetts eight, Rhode-Island and Providence Plantations one, Connecticut five, New-York six, New Jersey four, Pennsylvania eight, Delaware one, Maryland six, Virginia ten, North Carolina five, South Carolina five, and Georgia three.

When vacancies happen in the Representation from any State, the Executive Authority thereof shall issue Writs of Election to fill such Vacancies.

The House of Representatives shall chuse their Speaker and other Officers; and shall have the sole Power of Impeachment.

Section. 3. The Senate of the United States shall be composed of two Senators from each State, *chosen by the Legislature thereof,* for six Years; and each Senator shall have one Vote.

Immediately after they shall be assembled in Consequence of the first Election, they shall be divided as equally as may be into three Classes. The Seats of the Senators of the first Class shall be vacated at the Expiration of the second Year, of the second Class at the Expiration of the fourth Year, and of the third Class at the Expiration of the sixth Year, so that one third may be chosen every second Year; *and if Vacancies happen by Resignation, or otherwise, during the Recess of the Legislature of any State, the Executive thereof may make temporary Appointments until the next Meeting of the Legislature, which shall then fill such Vacancies.* No Person shall be a Senator who shall not have attained to the Age of thirty Years, and been nine Years a Citizen of the United States, and who shall not, when elected, be an Inhabitant of that State for which he shall be chosen.

The Vice President of the United States shall be President of the Senate, but shall have no Vote, unless they be equally divided.

The Senate shall chuse their other Officers, and also a President pro tempore, in the Absence of the Vice President, or when he shall exercise the Office of President of the United States.

The Senate shall have the sole Power to try all Impeachments. When sitting for that Purpose, they shall be on Oath or Affirmation. When the President of the United States is tried, the Chief Justice shall preside: And no Person shall be convicted without the Concurrence of two thirds of the Members present.

Judgment in Cases of Impeachment shall not extend further than to removal from Office, and disqualification to hold and enjoy any Office of honor, Trust or Profit under the United States: but the Party convicted shall nevertheless be liable and subject to Indictment, Trial, Judgment and Punishment, according to Law.

Section. 4. The Times, Places and Manner of holding Elections for Senators and Representatives, shall be prescribed in each State by the Legislature thereof; but the Congress may at any time by Law make or alter such Regulations, except as to the Places of chusing Senators.

The Congress shall assemble at least once in every Year, *and such Meeting shall be on the first Monday in December* unless they shall by Law appoint a different Day.

Section. 5. Each House shall be the Judge of the Elections, Returns and Qualifications of its own Members, and a Majority of each shall constitute a Quorum to do Business; but a smaller Number may adjourn from day to day, and may be authorized to compel the Attendance of absent Members, in such Manner, and under such Penalties as each House may provide.

Each House may determine the Rules of its Proceedings, punish its Members for disorderly Behaviour, and, with the Concurrence of two thirds, expel a Member.

Each House shall keep a Journal of its Proceedings, and from time to time publish the same, excepting such Parts as may in their Judgment require Secrecy; and the Yeas and Nays of the Members of either House on any question shall, at the Desire of one fifth of those Present, be entered on the Journal.

Neither House, during the Session of Congress, shall, without the Consent of the other, adjourn for more than three days, nor to any other Place than that in which the two Houses shall be sitting.

Section. 6. The Senators and Representatives shall receive a Compensation for their Services, to be ascertained by Law, and paid out of the Treasury of the United States. They shall in all Cases, except Treason, Felony and Breach of the Peace, be privileged from Arrest during their Attendance at the Session of their respective Houses, and in going to and returning from the same; and for any Speech or Debate in either House, they shall not be questioned in any other Place.

No Senator or Representative shall, during the Time for which he was elected, be appointed to any civil Office under the Authority of the United States, which shall have been created, or the Emoluments whereof shall have been encreased during such time; and no Person holding any Office under the United States, shall be a Member of either House during his Continuance in Office.

Section. 7. All Bills for raising Revenue shall originate in the House of Representatives; but the Senate may propose or concur with Amendments as on other Bills.

Every Bill which shall have passed the House of Representatives and the Senate, shall, before it become a Law, be presented to the President of the United States; If he approve he shall sign it, but if not he shall return it, with his Objections to that House in which it shall have originated, who shall enter the Objections at large on their Journal, and proceed to reconsider it. If after such Reconsideration two thirds of that House shall agree to pass the Bill, it shall be sent, together with the Objections, to the other House, by which it shall likewise be reconsidered, and if approved by two thirds of that House, it shall become a Law. But in all such Cases the Votes of both Houses shall be determined by yeas and Nays, and the Names of the Persons voting for and against the Bill shall be entered on the Journal of each House respectively. If any Bill shall not be returned by the President within ten Days (Sundays excepted) after it shall have been presented to him, the Same shall be a Law, in like Manner as if he had signed it, unless the Congress by their Adjournment prevent its Return, in which Case it shall not be a Law.

Every Order, Resolution, or Vote to which the Concurrence of the Senate and House of Representatives may be necessary (except on a question of Adjournment) shall be presented to the President of the United States; and before the Same shall take Effect, shall be approved by him, or being disapproved by him, shall be repassed by two thirds of the Senate and House of Representatives, according to the Rules and Limitations prescribed in the Case of a Bill.

Section. 8. The Congress shall have Power To lay and collect Taxes, Duties, Imposts and Excises, to pay the Debts and provide for the common Defence and general Welfare of the United States; but all Duties, Imposts and Excises shall be uniform throughout the United States;

To borrow Money on the credit of the United States;

To regulate Commerce with foreign Nations, and among the several States, and with the Indian Tribes;

To establish an uniform Rule of Naturalization, and uniform Laws on the subject of Bankruptcies throughout the United States;

To coin Money, regulate the Value thereof, and of foreign Coin, and fix the Standard of Weights and Measures;

To provide for the Punishment of counterfeiting the Securities and current Coin of the United States;

To establish Post Offices and post Roads;

To promote the Progress of Science and useful Arts, by securing for limited Times to Authors and Inventors the exclusive Right to their respective Writings and Discoveries;

To constitute Tribunals inferior to the supreme Court;

To define and punish Piracies and Felonies committed on the high Seas, and Offences against the Law of Nations;

To declare War, grant Letters of Marque and Reprisal, and make Rules concerning Captures on Land and Water;

To raise and support Armies, but no Appropriation of Money to that Uuse shall be for a longer Term than two Years;

To provide and maintain a Navy;

To make Rules for the Government and Regulation of the land and naval Forces;

To provide for calling forth the Militia to execute the Laws of the Union, suppress Insurrections and repel Invasions;

To provide for organizing, arming, and disciplining, the Militia, and for governing such Part of them as may be employed in the Service of the United States, reserving to the States respectively, the Appointment of the Officers, and the Authority of training the Militia according to the discipline prescribed by Congress;

To exercise exclusive Legislation in all Cases whatsoever, over such District (not exceeding ten Miles square) as may, by Cession of particular States, and the Acceptance of Congress, become the Seat of the Government of the United States, and to exercise like Authority over all Places purchased by the Consent of the Legislature of the State in which the Same shall be, for the Erection of Forts, Magazines, Arsenals, dock-Yards, and other needful Buildings; —And

To make all Laws which shall be necessary and proper for carrying into Execution the foregoing Powers, and all other Powers vested by this Constitution in the Government of the United States, or in any Department or Officer thereof.

Section. 9. The Migration or Importation of such Persons as any of the States now existing shall think proper to admit, shall not be prohibited by the Congress prior to the Year one thousand eight hundred and eight, but a Tax or duty may be imposed on such Importation, not exceeding ten dollars for each Person.

The Privilege of the Writ of Habeas Corpus shall not be suspended, unless when in Cases of Rebellion or Invasion the public Safety may require it.

No Bill of Attainder or ex post facto Law shall be passed.

No Capitation, or other direct, Tax shall be laid, unless in Proportion to the Census or Enumeration herein before directed to be taken.

No Tax or Duty shall be laid on Articles exported from any State.

No Preference shall be given by any Regulation of Commerce or Revenue to the Ports of one State over those of another; nor shall Vessels bound to, or from, one State, be obliged to enter, clear, or pay Duties in another.

No Money shall be drawn from the Treasury, but in Consequence of Appropriations made by Law; and a regular Statement and Account of the Receipts and Expenditures of all public Money shall be published from time to time.

No Title of Nobility shall be granted by the United States: And no Person holding any Office of Profit or Trust under them, shall, without the Consent of the Congress, accept of any present, Emolument, Office, or Title, of any kind whatever, from any King, Prince, or foreign State.

Section. 10. No State shall enter into any Treaty, Alliance, or Confederation; grant Letters of Marque and Reprisal; coin Money; emit Bills of Credit; make any Thing but gold and silver Coin a Tender in Payment of Debts; pass any Bill of Attainder, ex post facto Law, or Law impairing the Obligation of Contracts, or grant any Title of Nobility.

No State shall, without the Consent of the Congress, lay any Imposts or Duties on Imports or Exports, except what may be absolutely necessary for executing it's inspection Laws; and the net Produce of all Duties and Imposts, laid by any State on Imports or Exports, shall be for the use of the Treasury of the

United States; and all such Laws shall be subject to the Revision and Controul of the Congress.

No State shall, without the Consent of Congress, lay any Duty of Tonnage, keep Troops, or Ships of War in time of Peace, enter into any Agreement or Compact with another State, or with a foreign Power, or engage in War, unless actually invaded, or in such imminent Danger as will not admit of delay.

Article. II.

Section. 1. The executive Power shall be vested in a President of the United States of America. He shall hold his Office during the Term of four Years, and, together with the Vice President, chosen for the same Term, be elected, as follows:

Each State shall appoint, in such Manner as the Legislature thereof may direct, a Number of Electors, equal to the whole Number of Senators and Representatives to which the State may be entitled in the Congress: but no Senator or Representative, or Person holding an Office of Trust or Profit under the United States, shall be appointed an Elector.

The Electors shall meet in their respective States, and vote by Ballot for two Persons, of whom one at least shall not be an Inhabitant of the same State with themselves. And they shall make a List of all the Persons voted for, and of the Number of Votes for each; which List they shall sign and certify, and transmit sealed to the Seat of the Government of the United States, directed to the President of the Senate. The President of the Senate shall, in the Presence of the Senate and House of Representatives, open all the Certificates, and the Votes shall then be counted. The Person having the greatest Number of Votes shall be the President, if such Number be a Majority of the whole Number of Electors appointed; and if there be more than one who have such Majority, and have an equal Number of Votes, then the House of Representatives shall immediately chuse by Ballot one of them for President; and if no Person have a Majority, then from the five highest on the List the said House shall in like Manner chuse the President. But in chusing the President, the Votes shall be taken by States, the Representation from each State having one Vote; a quorum for this Purpose shall consist of a Member or Members from two thirds of the States, and a Majority of all the States shall be necessary to a Choice. In every Case, after the Choice of the President, the Person having the greatest Number of Votes of the Electors shall be the Vice President. But if there should remain two or more who have equal Votes, the Senate shall chuse from them by Ballot the Vice President.

The Congress may determine the Time of chusing the Electors, and the Day on which they shall give their Votes; which Day shall be the same throughout the United States.

No Person except a natural born Citizen, or a Citizen of the United States, at the time of the Adoption of this Constitution, shall be eligible to the Office of President; neither shall any Person be eligible to that Office who shall not have attained to the Age of thirty five Years, and been fourteen Years a Resident within the United States.

In Case of the Removal of the President from Office, or of his Death, Resignation, or Inability to discharge the Powers and Duties of the said Office, the Same shall devolve on the Vice President, and the Congress may by Law provide for the Case of Removal, Death, Resignation or Inability, both of the President and Vice President, declaring what Officer shall then act as President, and such Officer shall act accordingly, until the Disability be removed, or a President shall be elected.

The President shall, at stated Times, receive for his Services, a Compensation, which shall neither be increased nor diminished during the Period for which he shall have been elected, and he shall not receive within that Period any other Emolument from the United States, or any of them.

Before he enter on the Execution of his Office, he shall take the following Oath or Affirmation:—"I do solemnly swear (or affirm) that I will faithfully execute the Office of President of the United States, and will to the best of my Ability, preserve, protect and defend the Constitution of the United States."

Section. 2. The President shall be Commander in Chief of the Army and Navy of the United States, and of the Militia of the several States, when called into the actual Service of the United States; he may require the Opinion, in writing, of the principal Officer in each of the executive Departments, upon any Subject relating to the Duties of their respective Offices, and he shall have Power to grant Reprieves and Pardons for Offences against the United States, except in Cases of Impeachment.

He shall have Power, by and with the Advice and Consent of the Senate, to make Treaties, provided two thirds of the Senators present concur; and he shall nominate, and by and with the Advice and Consent of the Senate, shall appoint Ambassadors, other public Ministers and Consuls, Judges of the supreme Court, and all other Officers of the United States, whose Appointments are not herein otherwise provided for, and which shall be established by Law: but the Congress may by Law vest the Appointment of such inferior Officers, as they think proper, in the President alone, in the Courts of Law, or in the Heads of Departments.

The President shall have Power to fill up all Vacancies that may happen during the Recess of the Senate, by granting Commissions which shall expire at the End of their next Session.

Section. 3. He shall from time to time give to the Congress Information of the State of the Union, and recommend to their Consideration such Measures as he shall judge necessary and expedient; he may, on extraordinary Occasions, convene both Houses, or either of them, and in Case of Disagreement between them, with Respect to the Time of Adjournment, he may adjourn them to such Time as he shall think proper; he shall receive Ambassadors and other public Ministers; he shall take Care that the Laws be faithfully executed, and shall Commission all the Officers of the United States.

Section. 4. The President, Vice President and all civil Officers of the United States, shall be removed from Office on Impeachment for, and Conviction of, Treason, Bribery, or other high Crimes and Misdemeanors.

Article. III.

Section. 1. The judicial Power of the United States shall be vested in one supreme Court, and in such inferior Courts as the Congress may from time to time ordain and establish. The Judges, both of the supreme and inferior Courts, shall hold their Offices during good Behaviour, and shall, at stated Times, receive for their Services a Compensation, which shall not be diminished during their Continuance in Office.

Section. 2. The judicial Power shall extend to all Cases, in Law and Equity, arising under this Constitution, the Laws of the United States, and Treaties made, or which shall be made, under their Authority; —to all Cases affecting Ambassadors, other public Ministers and Consuls; —to all Cases of admiralty and maritime Jurisdiction; —to Controversies to which the United States shall be a Party; —to Controversies between two or more States; —*between a State and Citizens of another State*; —between Citizens of different States; —between Citizens of the same State claiming Lands under Grants of different States, and between a State, or the Citizens thereof, and foreign States, Citizens or Subjects.

In all Cases affecting Ambassadors, other public Ministers and Consuls, and those in which a State shall be Party, the supreme Court shall have original Jurisdiction. In all the other Cases before mentioned, the supreme Court shall have appellate Jurisdiction, both as to Law and Fact, with such Exceptions, and under such Regulations as the Congress shall make.

The Trial of all Crimes, except in Cases of Impeachment, shall be by Jury; and such Trial shall be held in the State where the said Crimes shall have been committed; but when not committed within any State, the Trial shall be at such Place or Places as the Congress may by Law have directed.

Section. 3. Treason against the United States shall consist only in levying War against them, or in adhering to their Enemies, giving them Aid and Comfort. No Person shall be convicted of Treason unless on the Testimony of two Witnesses to the same overt Act, or on Confession in open Court.

The Congress shall have Power to declare the Punishment of Treason, but no Attainder of Treason shall work Corruption of Blood, or Forfeiture except during the Life of the Person attainted.

Article. IV.

Section. 1. Full Faith and Credit shall be given in each State to the public Acts, Records, and judicial Proceedings of every other State. And the Congress may by general Laws prescribe the Manner in which such Acts, Records and Proceedings shall be proved, and the Effect thereof.

Section. 2. The Citizens of each State shall be entitled to all Privileges and Immunities of Citizens in the several States.

A Person charged in any State with Treason, Felony, or other Crime, who shall flee from Justice, and be found in another State, shall on Demand of the executive Authority of the State from which he fled, be delivered up, to be removed to the State having Jurisdiction of the Crime.

No Person held to Service or Labour in one State, under the Laws thereof, escaping into another, shall, in Consequence of any Law or Regulation therein, be discharged from such Service or Labour, but shall be delivered up on Claim of the Party to whom such Service or Labour may be due.

Section. 3. New States may be admitted by the Congress into this Union; but no new State shall be formed or erected within the Jurisdiction of any other State; nor any State be formed by the Junction of two or more States, or Parts of States, without the

Consent of the Legislatures of the States concerned as well as of the Congress.

The Congress shall have Power to dispose of and make all needful Rules and Regulations respecting the Territory or other Property belonging to the United States; and nothing in this Constitution shall be so construed as to Prejudice any Claims of the United States, or of any particular State.

Section. 4. The United States shall guarantee to every State in this Union a Republican Form of Government, and shall protect each of them against Invasion; and on Application of the Legislature, or of the Executive (when the Legislature cannot be convened), against domestic Violence.

Article. V.

The Congress, whenever two thirds of both Houses shall deem it necessary, shall propose Amendments to this Constitution, or, on the Application of the Legislatures of two thirds of the several States, shall call a Convention for proposing Amendments, which, in either Case, shall be valid to all Intents and Purposes, as Part of this Constitution, when ratified by the Legislatures of three fourths of the several States, or by Conventions in three fourths thereof, as the one or the other Mode of Ratification may be proposed by the Congress; Provided that no Amendment which may be made prior to the Year One thousA.nd eight hundred and eight shall in any Manner affect the first and fourth Clauses in the Ninth Section of the first Article; *and that no State, without its Consent, shall be deprived of its equal Suffrage in the Senate.*

Article. VI.

All Debts contracted and Engagements entered into, before the Adoption of this Constitution, shall be as valid against the United States under this Constitution, as under the Confederation.

This Constitution, and the Laws of the United States which shall be made in Pursuance thereof; and all Treaties made, or which shall be made, under the Authority of the United States, shall be the supreme Law of the Land; and the Judges in every State shall be bound thereby, any Thing in the Constitution or Laws of any State to the Contrary notwithstanding.

The Senators and Representatives before mentioned, and the Members of the several State Legislatures, and all executive and judicial Officers, both of the United States and of the several States, shall be bound by Oath or Affirmation, to support this Constitution; but no religious Test shall ever be required as a Qualification to any Office or public Trust under the United States.

Article. VII.
The Ratification of the Conventions of nine States, shall be sufficient for the Establishment of this Constitution between the States so ratifying the Same.
Attest William Jackson
Secretary

Done in Convention by the Unanimous Consent of the States present the Seventeenth Day of September in the Year of our Lord one thousA.nd seven hundred and Eighty seven and of the Independence of the United States of America the Twelfth In witness whereof We have hereunto subscribed our Names,
Go. WASHINGTON—Presidt. and deputy from Virginia
New Hampshire {
    JOHN LANGDON
    NICHOLAS GILMAN
Massachusetts {
    NATHANIEL GORHAM
    RUFUS KING
Connecticut {
    WM. SAML. JOHNSON
    ROGER SHERMAN
New York ...
    ALEXANDER HAMILTON
New Jersey {

WIL: LIVINGSTON
DAVID BREARLEY.
WM. PATERSON.
JONA: DAYTON
Pennsylvania {
  B FRANKLIN
  THOMAS MIFFLIN
  ROBT MORRIS
  GEO. CLYMER
  THOS. FITZ SIMONS
  JARED INGERSOLL
  JAMES WILSON
  GOUV MORRIS
Delaware {
  GEO: READ
  GUNNING BEDFORD jun
  JOHN DICKINSON
  RICHARD BASSETT
  JACO: BROOM
Maryland {
  JAMES MCHENRY
  DAN OF ST THOS. JENIFER
  DANL CARROLL
Virginia {
  JOHN BLAIR
  JAMES MADISON jr
North Carolina {
  WM. BLOUNT
  RICHD. DOBBS SPAIGHT
  HU WILLIAMSON
South Carolina {
  J. RUTLEDGE
  CHARLES COTESWORTH PINCKNEY
  CHARLES PINCKNEY
  PIERCE BUTLER
Georgia {
  WILLIAM FEW

ABR BALDWIN

In Convention Monday, September 17th, 1787

Present

The States of

New Hampshire, Massachusetts, Connecticut, MR. Hamilton from New York, New Jersey, Pennsylvania, Delaware, Maryland, Virginia, North Carolina, South Carolina and Georgia.

Resolved,

That the preceding Constitution be laid before the United States in Congress assembled, and that it is the Opinion of this Convention, that it should afterwards be submitted to a Convention of Delegates, chosen in each State by the People thereof, under the Recommendation of its Legislature, for their Assent and Ratification; and that each Convention assenting to, and ratifying the Same, should give Notice thereof to the United States in Congress assembled. Resolved, That it is the Opinion of this Convention, that as soon as the Conventions of nine States shall have ratified this Constitution, the United States in Congress assembled should fix a Day on which Electors should be appointed by the States which have ratified the same, and a Day on which the Electors should assemble to vote for the President, and the Time and Place for commencing Proceedings under this Constitution. That after such Publication the Electors should be appointed, and the Senators and Representatives elected: That the Electors should meet on the Day fixed for the Election of the President, and should transmit their Votes certified, signed, sealed and directed, as the Constitution requires, to the Secretary of the United States in Congress assembled, that the Senators and Representatives should convene at the Time and Place assigned; that the Senators should appoint a President of the Senate, for the sole purpose of receiving, opening and counting the Votes for President; and, that after he shall be chosen, the Congress, together with the President, should, without Delay, proceed to execute this Constitution.

By the Unanimous Order of the Convention

Go. WASHINGTON—President.

W. JACKSON Secretary.

Amendments to the Constitution of the United States (First Amended June 1791)

#	Amendments	Proposal Date	Enactment Date
1st	Citizens have the rights to freedom of religion, of speech, of the press, to petition the government about grievances, and to assemble	September 29, 1789	December 15, 1791
2nd	Citizen rights to keep and to bear arms	September 25, 1789	December 15, 1791
3rd	No quartering of soldiers in private houses during times of peace or war without citizens' consent or legal procedures	September 25, 1789	December 15, 1791
4th	Citizen rights against unreasonable searches and seizures and requirements for legal search warrants	September 25, 1789	December 15, 1791
5th	Citizen rights to grand jury indictments, to protection of due process, protection against self-incrimination and double jeopardy, and to fair market value in Eminent domain	September 25, 1789	December 15, 1791
6th	Citizen rights to a speedy and fair public trial by peers, to identification of accusers and accusations, to being able to confront one's accuser and subpoenaswitnesses, right to counsel, etc.	September 25, 1789	December 15, 1791
7th	Right to trial by jury, if requested, in civil cases	September 25, 1789	December 15, 1791
8th	No excessive bail, fines, or cruel and unusual punishment to citizens	September 25, 1789	December 15, 1791
9th	Citizens retain natural rights not identified in the Constitution	September 25, 1789	December 15, 1791
10th	Reserves rights to the states not specifically designated by the Constitution to the federal government	September 25, 1789	December 15, 1791
11th	Establishes the immunity of states from suits filed by out-of-state citizens and foreigners who are not living within state borders. Lays the foundation for sovereign immunity for the state and federal governments.	March 4, 1794	February 7, 1795
12th	Revises the process of electing the President of the U.S.A.	December 9, 1803	June 15, 1804
13th	Abolishes slavery in the U.S.A., except as punishment for a crime	January 31, 1865	December 6, 1865

	Description		
14th	The longest amendment. It approves citizenship for former slaves, establishes state due process, applies the Bill of Rights to state action, revises the apportionment of state representatives, and mandates that anyone who has rebelled against the United States is prohibited from public office	June 13, 1866	July 9, 1868
15th	The rights of citizens to vote shall not be restricted by race or previous condition of servitude	February 26, 1869	February 3, 1870
16th	Establishes the authority for the IRS and federal income tax	July 12, 1909	February 3, 1913
17th	Changes the way U.S. senators are elected from state legislatures to direct election by the citizens in each state	May 13, 1912	April 8, 1913
18th	Prohibition of the manufacture, sale, and distribution of alcoholic beverages	December 18, 1917	January 16, 1919
19th	Granting women the right to vote—Women's Suffrage	June 4, 1919	August 18, 1920
20th	Changing the time for Congress to begin a new session (Jan. 3) and for the president to begin a new administration (Jan. 20.)	March 2, 1932	January 23, 1933
21st	Repeal of the Eighteenth Amendment, which prohibited state and local manufacture and sale of alcohol	February 20, 1933	December 5, 1933
22nd	Term limits for the President of the U.S.A.—Only two 4-year terms allowed	March 24, 1947	February 27, 1951
23rd	Allowing Washington, D.C. citizens to choose a small number of electors for the Electoral College	June 16, 1960	March 29, 1961
24th	Non-payment of poll taxes outlawed as a way of restricting the voting rights of citizens	September 14, 1962	January 23, 1964
25th	New rules of presidential succession	July 6, 1965	February 10, 1967
26th	Voting age requirement established as 18 in the U.S.A.	March 23, 1971	July 1, 1971
27th	Allows the changing of congressional salaries and benefits	September 25, 1789	May 7, 1992

Important Proposed Amendments That Never Got Ratified

Amendment	Date Proposed	Status	Subject
Amendment for Congressional Apportionment	September 25, 1789	Though this issue has been made moot by time, circumstances, and experience, it was never rescinded and is thus technically alive and pending before state legislatures.	That state apportionment of U.S. members of the House of Representatives shall be based on population
Amendment to Prohibit Titles of Nobility Being Granted by Congress	May 1, 1810	This issue was never rescinded or made moot by another amendment, so technically it is still alive and pending before state legislatures.	Congress cannot issue or approve titles of nobility to American citizens.
Corwin Amendment on Preserving Slavery	March 2, 1861	This proposed amendment was never rescinded, but was made moot by the passage and ratification of the 13th amendment	To preserve slavery in all states that vote to retain it.
Amendment on Regulating Child Labor	June 2, 1924	This proposed amendment was never rescinded and is thus still an issue before state legislatures, although there are several more states now.	Congressional power to regulate the employment and conditions of employment for citizens under 18 years of age
The Equal Rights Amendment	March 22, 1972	Expired by 1982	Prohibition of inequality based on sex or gender
Voting Rights Amendment for the District of Columbia	August 22, 1978	Expired by 1986	Voting Rights in Congress for Washington, D.C.

Facts to Remember—African Americans and the U.S. Constitution

1. The 13th Amendment (1865), made the Fugitive Slave clause (Article 4, Section 2) null and void. This amendment ended slavery in America, not President Lincoln's Emancipation Proclamation.

2. The 14th Amendment, originally designed to provide citizenship to Black Americans, overturned the three fifths compromise clause (Article I, Section 2).

3. The 15th Amendment provided Black Americans and others the right to vote, but not the exercisable freedom to vote. That occurred with the 1965 Voting Rights Act.

Chapter Seven

Civil Rights and Liberties: Definitions, Discussion, and Case Studies

Civil Liberties

Civil liberties are legal rights guaranteed for individuals within a society. In America, these rights, or entitlements, are generally written in the amendments to the U.S. Constitution, and they are usually repeated in state constitutions. The fundamental civil liberties of Americans include freedom of speech and expression, protection against unreasonable searches and seizures, and other rights that are written in the Bill of Rights (the first ten amendments), the 13th, 14th, 15th and 19th amendments to the U.S. Constitution.

Influential Points to Remember

1. None of these civil liberties was contained in the original U.S. Constitution (America's second Constitution) ratified in 1788–1789. A compromise agreement between the Federalists (who advocated the strong central government of the new Constitution) and the Anti-Federalists, produced the Bill of Rights, which was summarized from the state constitutions of the thirteen original signers of the Declaration of Independence, and added to the U.S. Constitution in 1791.
2. The primary aim of the Bill of Rights was to protect American citizens from the abuses of the national government.

3. The amendment that provided individual citizen protection against state governments was the 14th Amendment.

4. None of the civil liberties is unlimited or absolute. Each, in fact, is quite limited and relative. It is the responsibility of the federal court system, including the U.S. Supreme Court, to define and interpret exactly what civil liberties mean in a dynamic world. What civil liberties meant in the 1850s is not necessarily what they mean currently.

5. Civil Liberties and Civil Rights can be referred to as Individual Rights and Group Rights. The Bill of Rights is the foundation for both.

6. The most basic—also called Fundamental—rights or liberties are the rights to free expression, and the rights to due process.

Civil Rights

Civil Rights in the U.S. can be defined as the guarantee that all groups of citizens have the right to equal protection of America's laws and equal access to public facilities and socio-economic-political opportunities in this country. Understandably, this is a *de jure*, or literal definition, rather than a *de facto*, or real-life one. That is, this is the ideal, not the fact of life in America. Also of note, having the right to do something or keep something is not the same as the freedom to exercise that right. The dynamic between possessing a legal right and having the freedom to exercise that right is fundamental to the evolution of civil rights and liberties in America.

Influential Points to Remember

1. Individual groups, including racial, ethnic, gender and sexual orientation, have had to learn how to fight effectively in order to receive rights that were supposed to be guaranteed. It has to be remembered that having legal rights granted provides no certainty that those rights will be protected or enforced. Civil rights/liberties does not equate to the automatic exercise of those civil rights/liberties.

2. The Civil Rights Movement was essentially about enforcing America's laws equally, and providing the same level and quality of treatment to all of America's citizens regardless of race, creed, color, gender, or previous conditions of servitude. The Civil Rights Movement used

methods of moral suasion, mass-based pressure, and civil disobedience of laws considered unjust, to force the issue. The 1964 Civil Rights Act (CRA), the 1965 Voting Rights Act (VRA), and their various amendments, all of which focus on enforcement legislation for laws already on the books (e.g., the 15th Amendment to the U.S. Constitution), are considered the crowning achievements of the Civil Rights Movement in America.

3. Based on interpretations by the Supreme Court, the principal amendment that provided individual citizen protection against state governments was the 14th. Theoretically, most American citizens now enjoy "substantial equality under the law." That is, legally, or *dejure*, housing discrimination has decreased markedly, citizens have equal access to facilities and accommodations (very few instances of white-colored signs remain), and citizens have an equal right to vote (although the exercise of that right stays in dispute since states have major control over it).

4. Legal equality is not equivalent to *de facto* equality. Depriving citizens of due process in law enforcement, in employment, in health care, in education, in housing accommodations, etc., is still traditionally practiced in America, particularly against racial, ethnic, gender, and sexual-orientation groups still disrespected, for the most part, in American society.

Political Values and Civil Rights

Black Americans and other peoples of color did not create this present political system in the U.S., although many of them did participate in providing the economic-social context within which it was created. The policy decisions that established the American political status quo were made by White men—mostly merchants, lawyers and slave owners—and the initial experimentation to adjust and to get the system to properly operate were also by them. Unfortunately, for the most part, Black Americans and other people of color were generally dismissed to the political margins through this early process.

Thus, the options available in this country to Blacks and other people of color (also gays, women, immigration rights activists, et al.) for gaining and maintaining full participation, leverage and respect within the American political system are packaged in four categories, all based on reaction and response.

a. Learning the system very well and how to work it is the first requirement, including learning the rules and the nuances.

b. Learning to skillfully and intelligently select those representatives who are entrusted to operate for your group's interests within this system is another critical requirement.

c. Learning to organize effectively, to build meaningful coalitions, and to vote consistently is a must. (Groups that cannot wield consistent clout at the ballot box or with large financial contributions to candidates are regularly disrespected and disregarded within the American system.)

d. Identifying, developing and utilizing the precise skills needed in order to get a group's interests regularly listened to and taken care of within this competitive environment, i.e., becoming politically competitive, is the final requirement. Learning how to effectively articulate, advocate and defend one's group interests is absolutely necessary in order to prevent being marginalized and continually taken for granted in this system.

The political values that make one competitive in America and that count the most have to do with group prestige, status, reputation and clout. There are favored ethnic and political groups, and there are less-favored groups according to a hierarchical ranking order developed early on in American society (sometimes called the Hierarchy of Ethnic Values [HEV]). The mainstream culture is based essentially on a White Anglo-Saxon Protestant model. All other groups have to respond, react to, comply with, acquiesce to, or resist that model. Either way, from that model comes most of our political values—what is politically effective, which groups will dominate and lead, whose interests will be taken care of first and most—and in order to get what we think we deserve from the system, we must become politically astute enough to understand and use those values for our own group benefit. Failure to do this will continue to result in disrespect and disregard by the political system in which we live.

The political theory of the HEV explains that every group other than the WASPs and their imitators will be adversely affected and badly treated in America for a time based on the negative public value associated with that group's possession of one or more accepted and ascribed characteristics. The group does not factually have to possess the characteristic (s), but just be perceived as possessing it. For example, Jews in America have regularly been blamed for being members of a group responsible for killing Jesus Christ, and for being solely interested in money and financial dominance, to the detriment of other people. Nevermind that those beliefs are stereotypes.

In the normal operation of American politics, people act more on what they believe, particularly about other groups or individuals, than what is actually true.

So Jews have been discriminated against in America for their religious beliefs and for some alleged past indiscretions. Jews have had to overcompensate for that adversity by finding positive components of American society that they could excel in and possibly control. The theory is that in order to reduce or eliminate the influence of one's negative socio-political position in America, one has to change one's reputation and status by acquiring an overwhelming body of positive American attributes. Out of a consistent accumulation of achievement in such positive activities (the public media, Hollywood, music industry, theater, higher education, medicine, business, etc.), Jews in America have expected to gain greater status, higher prestige, and a reputation for great American contributions, and they have done so. Every ethnic group other than WASPS has had to engage in that same process in order to change their negative value in American society.

That plan has worked for Jews in America, for the most part. Similarly it has eventually worked for the Irish, the Italians, the Vietnamese, Japanese, Koreans, Filipinos, and, lately, the Chinese. It has not yet worked for Latinos and for Blacks (in spite of the election of the first African American President of the United States recently).

However, that's the name of the political game we are in: live, learn, adapt, assert, get very prepared, and don't back off one's group interests. Find the components that will make one's group stronger and more respected, work hard to acquire or achieve them, or otherwise get ready to simply accept being constantly played by everybody else in America based on prior perceptions and stereotypes.

Selected List of Important Court Cases Dealing with the Legal Interpretations of Civil Liberties and Civil Rights

1. *Gibbons v. Ogden* (1824)

Both Aaron Ogden and Thomas Gibbons had permits to operate a commercial steamboat on the waters between New York and New Jersey. Ogden's permit came from the state of New York, and Gibbons' came from the U.S. government. In the legal cases they filed against each other, the Supreme Court eventually ruled that Gibbons' right to navigate the waters was tantamount, since his permit came from the federal government, and any time federal law and state law come into conflict over the matter of commerce, federal law will take precedence. According to the Constitution, only Congress has the power to regulate interstate commerce, and commerce here meant steamboat activity and any other such enterprise.

2. *Dred Scott v. Sanford* (1857)

As a slave, Dred Scott was taken by his master from Missouri, which was a slave state, to reside in a free state for several years, and then back to Missouri. With the help of several abolitionists, Scott sued his master for freedom, claiming that his residence in a free territory made him no longer a slave. With Chief Justice Roger Taney writing the majority opinion in a 7–2 vote, the Supreme Court ruled that Congress did not have the power to prohibit slavery in the territories, thus the Missouri Compromise of 1820 was unconstitutional, that since slaves and all Blacks living in the U.S. were not and could not ever be citizens, they could not testify or sue anybody in court.

3. *Plessy v. Ferguson* (1896)

Homer Ferguson, a very light-skinned African American living in Louisiana, challenged the state law that required separate accommodations on railroads for White and Black passengers. He sat in the White area of the train, identified himself as a Black man, and refused to move to the "Jim Crow" car as ordered by the conductor. He was arrested, and he sued the railroad and the state of Louisiana for violating his 13th and 14th Amendment rights. Eventually getting to the Supreme Court, a 7–1 majority ruled against him and upheld the Louisiana state law and its "separate but equal" doctrine.

4. *Schenck v. United States* (1919)

The U.S. drafted soldiers during WWI and passed the Espionage Act, which made it illegal for citizens to do anything that obstructed the war effort. As general secretary of the Socialist Party at the time, Charles Schenck was arrested and charged with conspiracy to print and circulate leaflets urging citizens to refuse to be drafted. Claiming that the Espionage Act violated his 1st Amendment rights to free speech, his case got to the Supreme Court, which ruled against him. Schenck argued that the Espionage Act violated his rights to freedom of speech and freedom of the press. The Court held that, based on the doctrine of "a clear and present danger" that the Court had created, in extraordinary circumstances such as war, Congress and government could override citizens' rights.

5. *Gitlow v. New York* (1925)

As a member of the American Socialist Party, Benjamin Gitlow authored two pamphlets that got him charged with and convicted of violating New York State's Criminal Anarchy Act of 1902. In his appeal, he argued that his 14th Amendment due process rights and his 1st Amendment rights to free speech and press were infringed upon by that New York law. The Supreme Court eventually ruled against him, but in this case the Court began the precedent-setting process of incorporating large segments of the Bill of Rights into cases that raised the 14th Amendment as an issue. This process led the Court to declare certain rights in the Bill of Rights as fundamental freedoms.

6. *Near v. Minnesota* (1931)

Jay Near and Howard Guilford, in 1927, published *The Saturday Press* newspaper, which accused several government officials and the police chief of Minneapolis, Minnesota of corruption, gangland activities, and other assorted evils. They were shot at and eventually closed down and arrested, charged with violating Minnesota's 1925 Public Nuisance Act. The case eventually was handled by the Supreme Court, and it ruled that the Minnesota law violated the 1st Amendment as applied through the 14th Amendment. State government was prohibited from imposing a "prior restraint" on freedom of the press and speech.

7. *Powell v. Alabama* (1932)

In the state of Alabama, seven young and poor African Americans were convicted in a one-day trial by an all-White jury of a false charge of rape involving two White girls. The youths could not afford and did not receive adequate counsel. The Supreme Court reversed the convictions, ordering a new trial and court-appointed defense attorneys, and for the first time said that the 14th Amendment guarantees of equal protection and due process applied in state courts as well as federal.

8. *Brown v. Board of Education of Topeka* (1954)

The class action case brought before the Supreme Court by the NAACP in which the Court reversed its earlier *Plessy v. Ferguson* (1896) ruling as applied to public education. In this case, the Court ruled that separate education is inherently unequal education and is a violation of equal protection and due process clauses of the 14th Amendment. One year later, the Court followed up that decision with an order to state and local school districts to create school desegregation plans to end separate education "with all deliberate speed."

9. *Mapp v. Ohio* (1961)

In Cleveland, Ohio, without first obtaining a warrant, police raided the home of a Cleveland resident, Ms. Mapp, confiscated boxes, papers, and pamphlets found there, and arrested her. She was convicted of possessing pornographic and obscene material and in the appeals process the Supreme Court ruled that the search and seizure by the police violated Ms. Mapp's 4th and 14th Amendment rights because they seized material without a proper search warrant. The Court stated its now-famous Exclusionary Rule that material taken illegally would be excluded as evidence against persons accused of crimes in state and federal courts.

10. *Engle v. Vitale* (1962)

For New York public schools, the governing body, the state Board of Regents, authorized the use of a short, voluntary prayer for pupils to recite at the start of each school day. The prayer was, "Almighty God, we acknowledge our dependence upon Thee, and beg Thy blessings upon U.S., our teachers, and our country." Eventually, the U.S. Supreme Court, in a 6–1 decision, ruled that the Board of Regents' authorization constituted a violation of the 1st Amendment's "establishment clause" against government sponsorship of any religious activity and could not be used. It was unconstitutional. This was the first in a long series of such rulings.

11. *Gideon v. Wainwright* (1963)

In Florida, Mr. Clarence Gideon was arrested and charged with a breaking and entering/theft felony. At his preliminary hearing, he requested, but was refused, a court-appointed attorney. At trial, he handled his own case and was convicted and sentenced to five years. On appeal, eventually to the Supreme Court, the ruling was that Gideon had the right to a court-appointed attorney as requested, based on the 14th Amendment and its incorporation of the 6th Amendment in this non-capital crime, non-federal case. This case, along with *Powell v. Alabama*, ushered in a whole series of interpretations regarding a citizen's right to counsel.

12. *Escobedo v. Illinois* (1964)

This case, involving the conviction of Mr. Danny Escobedo for shooting and killing his brother-in-law, brought in the issue of when a suspect held by police had a right to an attorney. This case was decided one year after the *Gideon v. Wainwright* ruling. In *Escobedo*, the Supreme Court overturned his conviction and ruled that Escobedo's confession was inadmissible because of a violation of the 6th Amendment guarantee of an attorney. This was the first major case in which the Court recognized a suspect's right to an attorney during police interrogation before an indictment, or in other words, from the time individuals become primary suspects they have a right to an attorney.

13. *Miranda v. Arizona* (1966)

The famous Miranda Rights case involved a Mr. Ernesto Miranda, a resident of the state of Arizona who was arrested and questioned for over two hours on suspicion of rape and kidnapping. He confessed, was convicted based largely on that evidence, and the case eventually was appealed to the Supreme Court. The ruling, in a 5–4 decision, reversed his conviction. The Court pronounced three primary guidelines related to this case: (a) An individual arrested or held by police for questioning has the right to speak to an attorney during such questioning and to have the attorney present throughout the interrogation. The person held by police must be informed by police of his or her right to counsel. (b) An individual held for such questioning who is not informed of this right cannot have any information obtained in the interrogation used against him or her at trial. (c) If the individual held lacks the resources to hire an attorney, the questioning must wait until the Court appoints an attorney for that individual. As now used regularly on TV and in the movies, the Miranda Rights statement used by law enforcement generally goes like this: "You have the right to remain silent. Anything you say can and will be used against you. You have the right to have an attorney present during questioning. If you cannot afford one, one will be appointed for you. Do you understand each and every one of these rights as they have been presented to you?"

14. *Harper v. Virginia Board of Elections* (1966)

As a result of a civil suit appeal, the Supreme Court ruled that a long-applied Virginia poll tax essentially used on African Americans trying to vote violated the 14th Amendment's "equal protection clause." This ruling paved the way for effectively eliminating racial and ethnic-focused restrictions on voting used by several states.

15. *In Re Gault* (1967)

After having already been placed on court-ordered probation, a 15-year-old boy named Gerald Francis Gault was later arrested and charged with making an obscene phone call, thus violating his probation. Law enforcement did not notify the young man's parents before arresting him and did not leave a notice that they had detained him. Mr. Gault was sent to state prison for juveniles, and on appeal the Supreme Court overturned his conviction. The Court ruled that the police violated the youth's 5th, 6th and 14th Amendment due process rights. The police and the Juvenile Court should have provided an adequate notice of the charges against the youth, should have notified both Mr. Gault and his parents that he had a right to counsel, should have provided an opportunity for confrontation and cross-examination at the hearings, and should have provided adequate safeguards against self-incrimination. This was the first major case in which all of these rights were summarily applied to juveniles as well as adults.

16. *Lemon v. Kurtzman* (1971)

In a conjoined group of cases collectively called *Lemon v.. Kurzman,* state government officials in Pennsylvania and Rhode Island were sued for using public funds to pay teacher salaries at parochial schools. The Supreme Court ruled unanimously, in a 7–0 decision, that direct government assistance to religious schools was unconstitutional. In this case, the Court created what is now known as the "Lemon Test" to decide if a law is in violation of the Establishment Clause of the 1st Amendment. The Lemon Test lays out three requirements, the violation of any one of them demonstrating that the government had indeed violated the public's right not to have religions established or sponsored by the state: (a) The government's action that is in question must have a demonstrated secular legislative purpose, (b) The resulting effect of the government's action must not advance or hinder religious practices, and (c) The results of government action must not be that the state creates "excessive government entanglement" with the practice of religion.

17. *Roe v. Wade* (1973)

In this famous abortion rights case, Jane Roe, a fictitious name for a pregnant Texas woman, challenged her state's anti-abortion laws on 14th Amendment due process grounds. The Supreme Court upheld Roe's claim that her property rights to privacy entitled her to an abortion if she chose one. The Court ruling also made clear that: (a) The state cannot limit abortions in the first three months of pregnancy except to require that abortions be performed by licensed physicians, (b) For the protection of the health of the mother, the state can step in to stipulate the conditions under which abortions may be performed during the second three months of pregnancy, and (c) The state is authorized to outlaw abortions, if it sees fit, after a woman is six months pregnant or more in order to protect the fetus.

18. *Regents of the University of California at Davis v. Bakke* (1978)

This is the precedent-setting reverse discrimination case. In it, Allan Bakke, a Vietnam veteran, sued the University of California, Davis Medical School for admission based on a claim that a racial quota system the university used to set aside sixteen admission slots for new minority students was a violation of the 14th Amendment's equal protection clause.

Eventually getting to the Supreme Court, the justices there agreed that Bakke must be admitted to the UC Davis medical school, in a 5–4 decision, but the Court also upheld the constitutionality of affirmative action in general. The Court stipulated that the University could consider race as a contributing factor in admission decisions, but that race could not be the only admissions criterion.

19. *Grutter v. Bollinger* (2003)

This was a follow-up affirmative action case in which a rejected White candidate for the University of Michigan Law School, sued for admission (Lee Bollinger was the president of the university at the time) based on the 14th Amendment. The Supreme Court, in a 5–4 vote, upheld the UM's affirmative action procedures and did not agree to admit the student.

20. *Griswold v. Connecticut* (1965)

This is a landmark Supreme Court case which held, in a 7–2 vote, that a Connecticut statue that prohibited the use of any drug by doctors to prevent conception, was unconstitutional based on an implied right of privacy in the U.S. Constitution (14th and 9th Amendments). This case set the legal precedent for the later abortion rights case, *Roe v. Wade* (1973). It also contained Justice John Marshall Harlan's elaboration of his famous explanation of substantive due process (as opposed to structural due process), that has been used by federal courts ever since. (This explanation was first used in *Poe v. Ullman* [1961] in a case that the Supreme Court dismissed.)

Especially after the 19th century, the African American fight for inclusion has focused on direct action and judicial pursuits, with congressional legislation as a secondary strategy. Below are the primary blocks to the judicial road forward.

Primary Supreme Court Cases Affecting the Civil Rights of African Americans

1857: In *Dred Scott v. Sanford*, Dred Scott, a slave in Missouri, sued for his freedom on the grounds that he had lived for a time in a "free" territory. The Court ruled against him. The Roger Taney majority opinion said that Scott's enslaved status continued regardless of having resided for a while in a free state—slaveowners could not be deprived of their property. Moreover, as a slave Scott had no right to testify in court and thus the action should never have been brought forth, and, more broadly, for all Blacks in the country, they were not and could not be citizens. And finally, "there were no rights the colored man has in America that Whites were bound to respect." This decision eviscerated the status of free Blacks in America.

1883: In combining three early civil rights cases, the Court ruled that the last one, the Civil Rights Act of 1875, was unconstitutional. This Act was the final legislative piece from the Reconstruction Congress, and promised equality of access in public accommodations, theaters, motels, transportation, etc. The Court's ruling meant that the federal government could not police private sector segregation.

1896: In *Plessy v. Ferguson*, the Court upheld a Louisiana state law that required restaurants, hotels, hospitals, and other public places to serve African Americans only in separate accommodations. This ruling broadly legalized Jim Crow segregation in America under the infamous "separate but equal" doctrine. The Court said that segregation is "universally recognized as within the competency of states in the exercise of their police powers."

1932: In *Powell v. Alabama*, the Supreme Court overturned the "Scottsboro Boys" convictions—a group of Black youths collectively found guilty by all-White juries of raping two White women—and guaranteed the right of free counsel for all American citizens in both state and federal courts in which they could not afford private counsel.

1938: In *Missouri ex el Gaines v. Canada*, the Supreme Court ruled that Missouri violated the equal protection clause of the 14th Amendment by prohibiting the plaintiff's admission to a state law school. Sending the plaintiff, an African American resident, to an out-of-state law school did not satisfy that equal protection obligation and Mr. Lionel Gaines, the plaintiff, was ordered admitted to the all-White University of Missouri School of Law by the Court. This case was the first step in the NAACP Legal Defense Fund's effort to have the separate-but-equal doctrine overturned.

1948: In *Shelley v. Kramer*, the Court ruled that the government could not constitutionally enforce a "restrictive covenant" that prevented Americans of certain race from owning or occupying property.

1950: In the *Sweatt v. Painter* and *McLaurin v. Oklahoma State Regents* cases, the Court ruled against the segregation of African American students in law and graduate schools in spite of the Plessy decision. With the help of the U.S. Justice Department, which filed a brief to the Court, arguing that *Plessy* was unconstitutional and should be overturned, the NAACP Legal Defense Fund lawyers, led by Thurgood Marshall, used these two cases and *Gaines* to map out a strategy that would eventually convince the Court to rule against the constitutionality of the separate-but-equal doctrine.

1954: In *Brown v. Board of Education*, the case that overturned *Plessy*, Chief Justice Earl Warren, reading his first major opinion from the bench, said: "We conclude, unanimously, that in the field of public education the doctrine of 'separate but equal' has no place. Separate educational facilities are inherently unequal."

1955: In *Brown v. Board II*, the second part of the Court's ruling, the Supreme Court ordered that the nation's public school systems must abolish their racially dual systems, but could do so "with all deliberate speed," which gave them far too much room for delay.

1956: The Supreme Court affirmed a lower court ruling that declared segregation of the Montgomery public bus system illegal, giving a major civil rights victory to Rosa Parks, Martin Luther King, Jr., E.D. Nixon, and the thousands of African Americans who had mounted a successful bus boycott, 1955–1956. This was the beginning of the modern Civil Rights Movement.

1958: In *Cooper v. Aaron*, the Supreme Court upheld its earlier ruling in *Brown v. Board,* and added that official resistance and community violence could not justify delays in implementing desegregation efforts.

1964: In this case, *Heart of Atlanta Motel, Inc. v. United States*, which challenged the constitutionality of the Civil Rights Act of 1964, the Court reaffirmed the legislation and held that the motel in question had no right "to select its guests as it sees fit, free from governmental regulation."

1967: In this ruling, *Loving v. Virginia*, the Court declared that the prohibition on interracial marriage was unconstitutional and illegal. The decision forced sixteen states that banned interracial marriage at that time to revise their laws.

1968: In *Jones v. Alfred H. Mayer Co.*, the Court reaffirmed the Civil Rights Act of 1866, which bans racial discrimination in housing by private and governmental housing providers.

1971: In *Swann v. Charlotte-Mecklenburg Board of Education*, the Court held that busing students into desegregated schools was appropriate to do to achieve the ruling in *Brown*.

1971: In *Griggs v. Duke Power Co.*, a major case in private employment, the Court held that Title VII of the 1964 Civil Rights Act not only outlawed overt, intentional job discrimination, it also prohibited employer practices that had a discriminatory effect on job applicants who were minorities or women. Specifically, the Court struck down tests and other employment practices that disproportionately screened out African American applicants for jobs at the Duke Power Company, especially when those tests could not be shown to be job-related.

1974: In *Milliken v. Bradley*, the Court shifted back to a states' rights position in education. In the Detroit metropolitan area, the Court effectively limited school busing to achieve desegregation to the boundary of a city's borders. In a 5–4 decision the Court struck down Detroit's city-suburb desegregation plan that required transporting students across school district boundaries. Even with evidence of Michigan state government's past and then-current school segregation practices, the Court concluded that "local control" was important to maintain in education and thus the local and state government should be granted some leeway in how they chose to achieve school desegregation.

1977: In *Milliken II*, the Court held that the state of Michigan, and the Detroit school system, had to devise and finance a plan to correct the educational deficits demonstrated by African American children. These deficits, the Court concluded, had been caused by long-term enforced segregation in the Michigan public schools and could not be eliminated merely by physical desegregation (busing).

1978: In *Regents of the University of California v. Bakke*, the first major judicial victory for advocates of "reverse discrimination," the Court struck down the U.C. medical school's special admissions program that set aside a fixed number of seats for minority applicants. Calling this an illegal quota, the Court ruled that the admissions program violated Title VI of the 1964 Civil Rights Act. In the majority opinion by Justice Powell, the Court concluded that race could lawfully be considered as one of several factors in making admissions decisions, and that lawful affirmative action programs in education may be based on reasons other than redressing past discrimination—e.g., a university's educational interest in attaining a diverse student body could appropriately justify an allowable affirmative action program.

1980: In *City of Mobile v. Bolden,* the Court again shifted to the states' rights position and narrowly interpreted both the 14th and 15th Amendments to the Constitution, and the Voting Rights Act of 1965. The Court held that, in order to establish that a voting rights violation had occurred, the federal government must prove "discriminatory intent" by voting officials or law-makers in making a change in voting practices and having those changes negatively impact minority voting access. Congress overturned this ruling two years later with the passage of the 1982 Amendments to the Voting Rights Act.

1984: In *Grove City v. Bell,* the Supreme Court gave a strange interpretation of the CRA's Title IX. In its conclusions, the majority opinion narrowly identified Title IX's protections against unequal treatment to only the single program within an institution that received federal funding, e.g., a college's financial aid department—but not the entire college or university. Using this viewpoint, the Court exonerated virtually all college athletic programs from compliance with Title IX, since athletic programs rarely received direct federal funding. This decision was legislatively overturned with the enactment of the Civil Rights Restoration Act in 1988.

1986: In *Wygant v. Jackson Board of Education,* in another "reverse discrimination" victory, the Court ruled that lawful affirmative action programs cannot lay off more senior White workers to protect the jobs of less senior Black workers.

1986: In *Meritor Savings Bank v. Vinson*, in a unanimous ruling, the Court held that sexual harassment is a form of unlawful job discrimination under Title VII of the 1964 Civil Rights Act.

1987: In *United States v. Paradise*, the Court upheld a one-for-one promotion requirement (i.e., for every White candidate promoted, a qualified African American would also be promoted) in the Alabama Department of Public Safety, finding it to be narrowly tailored and necessary to eliminate the effects of Alabama's long-term discrimination that the lower court had found "blatant and continuous."

1988: In *Lyng v. Northwest Indian Cemetery Protection*, the Supreme Court ruled that the construction of a Forest Service road through an ancient site held sacred by several tribes did not infringe upon the tribes' constitutionally protected religious freedoms.

1989: In *City of Richmond v. Croson*, the Court for the first time used the "strict scrutiny doctrine" to evaluate the legality of an affirmative action plan to correct previous discriminatory practices. With this standard, the Court struck down Richmond, Virginia's local ordinance that established a minority business set-aside program. In this case, the Court, for the first time, adopted the strict scrutiny standard of review in assessing affirmative action programs. "Strict scrutiny," as defined by the Court, demands that affirmative action programs be based—not on a race-conscious remedy—but on a "compelling government interest" and that the programs be narrowly tailored to ensure that the programs fit that interest. Strict scrutiny has now become the dominant standard used in most affirmative action cases.

1989: In *Patterson v. McLean Credit Union*, the Court held that the Civil Rights Act of 1866 covered only job discrimination at the hiring stage and provided no authority to address racial harassment and other forms of discrimination once a worker was on the job. This ruling and others similar to it were legislatively overturned by the passage of the *1991 Civil Rights Act*.

1993: In *Shaw v. Reno*, the Supreme Court ruled that it was illegal to use race in formulating legislative redistricting plans aimed at creating a voting district likely to elect a member of a minority group. By a 5–4 vote, the Court struck down North Carolina's 12th Congressional District plan that allowed the first election of an African American member of Congress since Reconstruction. The Court ruled that districts cannot be so "bizarrely shaped" that they can violate the rights of White voters.

1995: In *Adarand Constructors v. Pena*, the Supreme Court extended its prior ruling in *Croson* and held that the strict scrutiny standard must also be applied to federal affirmative action programs. The Court, however, did not bar affirmative action programs that were properly designed.

2003: In *Grutter v. Bollinger*, the Court made this case the primary current precedent for affirmative action cases in education. In it, the court more explicitly lays out the strict scrutiny standard to be used in public education affirmative action situations, but reaffirms that affirmative action plans properly written, in which race or ethnicity is but one factor among several used to make admissions and other decisions, can still be allowable. Strict scrutiny in *Grutter* meant a "highly individualized, holistic review of each applicant's admissions file," in which race or ethnicity was not considered as a factor in a "mechanical way."

2013: In a 5–4 majority decision written by Chief Justice John Roberts, the U.S. Supreme Court struck down as unconstitutional Title IV of the VRA, saying that the formula used to determine which states had to obtain pre-clearance before making changes in their voting practices was out-of-date and based on old data, thereby violating the 14th Amendment's equal protection clause. The Court ruled that the formula must be re-written before it can be used again by the government to prevent voting discrimination against minorities. Although decried in the media as having eviscerated the VRA, this decision did not invalidate the VRA, but it did make it more difficult to apply.

Many scholars of African American involvement in the American political system see the beginning of serious Black American political activity around 1870, in the aftermath of the passage of the 14th Amendment and the election of Senator Hiram Revels in Mississippi as the first African American member of Congress (John W. Menard of Louisiana was actually elected first, in 1868, but his legislative colleagues would not allow him to take his congressional seat).

As a matter of political historical fact, however, beyond the election results and legislative attainments related to African Americans in politics, the single most important catalyst and spur forward for African American political involvement was and is Black community organizations, or non-governmental organizations (NGOs). There were innumerable groups starting, stopping, expanding, dying, forming alliances, and struggling alone. It has been their accumulated collective successes that have been the engine forward for Black America.

Chief among these groups were:

A. The Free African Society, established in 1787. As mentioned in Chapter 3, the FAS was formed as a religious-based mutual-aid and Black business network association that provided the foundation for the first national Black church—the African Methodist Episcopal Church—and the first Black insurance companies. It also established the free Black middle class in an organizational setting, with its mantra, "We are Americans, and we are bound to be equal."

B. The General Colored Association of Massachusetts, 1826, formed to support race progress and to agitate for the termination of slavery in the USA. (Other Black American-led abolitionist groups, 1788–1850, included the African Abolition Freehold Society, the African Female Anti-Slavery Society, the New York Committee of Vigilance, the Negro Union of Newport, the African Union Society of Newport.) These groups petitioned Congress, lectured widely, held protest marches, wrote newspaper articles, and otherwise advocated the end of slavery and race discrimination. Some of them openly advocated the mass exodus of African Americans to Africa, Haiti, or Central America in colonization schemes, such as the Liberian Exodus Joint Stock Company of 1877.

C. The Free Colored Convention Movement, 1830–1864. At its first meeting in Philadelphia with 40 delegates elected from Black communities in nine different states, including two African American women, this gathering created the first national Black political organization, the American Society of Free People of Color. Its combined aims were to improve the status and condition of colored people in the U.S.A., including agitating for the ending of slavery and creating a communications network for employment, crisis response, etc.; to prepare and support mass migration of African American families especially to Canada; and to be the political voice of Black Americans at the local, state, and national levels. Meeting annually, the organization effectively disbanded after the passage of the 13th Amendment, and the last convention was held in Syracuse, New York, in 1864.

D. The Ex-Slave Mutual Relief, Bounty, and Pension Association (aka, the Ex-Slave Pension Movement), started in 1894 in south Nashville, Tennessee, by Mrs. Callie House and the Reverend Isaiah Dickerson in the aftermath of the passage of the 14th Amendment. This was the first full-scale national reparations organization created in the U.S.A. by Black Americans. It had a national structure, with state and local chapters, supported by membership dues. Its aims were to care for the sick and disabled among its membership, to provide burial expenses for departed members, and to lobby and advocate relentlessly for the passage of congressional legislation that supported the ex-slave reparations project based on the system then in use for providing pensions to military veterans. Pension Movement organizers traveled all over the South in attempts to recruit ex-slaves. Eventually, elements of the federal government took opposition to the Movement's efforts, and after over ten years of surveillance and investigation, the government indicted Callie House and thirteen other national officers. On the flimsiest of evidence, the government convicted Mrs. House and sentenced her to one year and a day. She was the only one convicted and imprisoned, and was released after several months on good behavior. The national reach of the organization dissolved after her trial, but local and state chapters of the Pension Movement continued operations well into the 1920s. The Ex-Slave Pension Movement was the foundation organization for the reparations movement in the U.S.A., but it never could get the congressional support necessary for an African American reparations bill.

E. Marcus Garvey's Universal Negro Improvement Association and African Communities League (UNIA-ACL). Started in 1914 in Jamaica, and 1916 in New York, this became the largest mass organization of African Americans in American history, eventually counting its regular membership in the millions. Mr. Garvey advocated a race-first, be-proud-to-be-Black agenda that included continuing preparations to create and build an African government outside the continent to be returned to Africa, triumphantly owning African land. In 1920, Mr. Garvey held the largest of his annual UNIA conventions in New York, a gathering of over 25,000 adherents, which lasted for 30 days. At that gathering, members agreed on creating a new Black government, agreed on the red-black-green flag (now used all over the Black world) as its symbol, agreed on a citizenship process, elected national officers, and agreed on a UNIA constitution. Mr. Garvey regularly published the newspaper, The Negro World, which he distributed as far away as Australia and South Africa, and he strongly advocated a modern Pan-African unification project called a "United States of Africa." He and his officers coordinated a number of Pan-African conferences, generally held in New York, and eventually he purchased several steam ships as part of the Black Star Line Shipping project to engage in international ocean-going commerce in support of the project of purchasing African land and developing a new African government for African Americans on that property. He came to the attention of the U.S. government, particularly to the Justice Department's J. Edgar Hoover. The Garvey issue was Mr. Hoover's first major case dealing with a popular Black leader, and Hoover eventually had Mr. Garvey discredited and arrested for mail fraud regarding the shipping line. Mr. Garvey was convicted on very flimsy evidence, sentenced, commuted, and deported. He died in London in 1940, but nearly a century later, his UNIA-ACL is still operating in the USA, parts of the Caribbean, and in Africa. He is recognized as a national hero of Jamaica and there is an annual Marcus Garvey Day celebration there and in other parts of the world around his August 17 birthday. The Garvey Movement influenced virtually every other Black Nationalist organization created subsequently in the U.S., including the Nation of Islam (NOI), the Black Panther Party for Self-Defense (BPPSD), the Black Student Union (BSU), Republic of New Africa (RNA), Revolutionary Action Movement (RAM), Black United Front (BUF), etc. The Garvey Movement also strongly influenced the African independence movement against colonialism, and became the major inspiration for Africa's first independent Black government in Ghana, 1957. The Ghanaian flag is red, black, green, and gold with a black star at its center.

F. The National Council of Negro Women was formed in 1935 as a response to a national call issued by Mary McLeod Bethune, the then-president of Bethune-Cookman College and the Minority Affairs Advisor to Franklin Roosevelt's administration. The call was answered by twenty-eight independent Black women's organizations to create a "national organization of national organizations" among them that could speak as one voice for African American women on matters of public policy that related to the quality of life and the political-economic opportunities available for Negro women and their families. Mary Church Terrell, one of the assembled leaders, suggested the formation of a Negro Women's Council, and the rest of the assemblage agreed. Since its inception, the NCNW has been a major participant in the Civil Rights Movement, it has become a major clearinghouse of information beneficial to the Black community, it has built a network of contacts to more than 10 million African American women and families, and it has become a highly respected voice of Black concerns, particularly through its chief spokesperson, long-time president Dorothy Height (who died in 2010).

G. The National Afro-American Association, formed in 1898, in Rochester, New York, became the first national civil rights organization for African Americans in the U.S.A. Formed as a non-profit organizational and rational response to increased, persistent lynchings of African Americans, and to the growing epidemic of state restrictions on Black American voting rights, the Council set up local, state, and national chapters that made activities reports in a national conference coordinated every year in a relatively large American city. Site examples included Chicago, Indianapolis, Louisville, St. Louis, Detroit, New York, and the last national meeting held in Baltimore, 1907. The Council was structured to allow full participation and voice by African American male and female leaders, which was a marked departure from other groups. There was a large national executive committee that included, constitutionally, at least one female leader from every American state or territory. The Council lobbied relentlessly for a federal anti-lynching law, and filed legal suits against Black voting restrictions. The Council also met regularly with then-U.S. President William McKinley and spoke as the primary political voice of the Black community. These meetings were regularly noted and reported on in the local newspapers, both mainstream and African American editions. Members of the Council included Council founder T. Thomas Fortune, the editor of the New York Age newspaper, both Dr. W. E. B. Dubois and Tuskegee Institute's Booker T. Washington, Ida Wells-Barnett, Mary Terrell Church, and the longest term president of the Council, A.M.E. Bishop Alexander Walters. The latter's leadership reiterated the strong umbilical cord between the Black Church and Black American political activities. Partially because many members felt that Booker T. Washington co-opted the Council, the Council was superseded in 1908 by the more activist Niagara Movement, and lost many of its members to that organization and to its contemporary, the newly formed NAACP.

H. The Niagara Movement was formed in 1905 by William Monroe Trotter and W. E. B. Dubois as a militant protest alternative to what they felt were conciliatory and accommodationist policies advocated by Booker T. Washington, who was at the time the single most influential Black American leader in the U.S.A. The Niagara Movement challenged segregationist Jim Crow laws and violence against Black Americans directly, with both public demonstrations and incisive public writing. The organization's Declaration of Principles specifically demanded an end to the convict lease system, which was widely recognized as an end-run around the 13th Amendment, and to increased economic opportunities and outright land ownership for Blacks in the South so that they could make a decent living and eliminate their dependence on White landowners through sharecropping and tenant farming, among other activities. The group's motto was to engage in political agitation repeatedly until the lives of African Americans were improved. As in the earlier National Afro-American Council, women's voices were invited and welcomed, but only after a major conflict over the issue between Dubois—who favored such equality—and Trotter, who opposed it. Mainly through Trotter's editorship of the Boston Guardian newspaper, the Movement also took on labor union discrimination against Black workers. The Niagara Movement organization eventually established over 25 local and state chapters, and it was through these chapters that the Movement did its best work. In Massachusetts and in Washington, D.C., Movement members successfully agitated for gains against racial discrimination. The organization collapsed at the national level, however, by 1910, after Trotter's resignation over continued fights with Dubois. The Bookerite followers of Booker T. Washington also did everything they could to undermine the organization and to diminish its influence. By 1910, the newly formed NAACP had siphoned off most of the active Black membership of the Niagara Movement, including W. E. B. Dubois, although Trotter stayed opposed to the multi-racial mix of that organization and never joined it. The Movement's last national gathering was 1909 in Sea Isle, New Jersey, after which it disbanded.

I. The National Association for the Advancement of Colored People (NAACP), was formed in 1910 by a coalition of White race relations groups and Black activists as a result of the 1908 race riot in Springfield, Illinois, and the continuing decline in the quality of life for African Americans in the country. The NAACP eventually became one of the most significant and important civil rights organizations of the 20th century, mainly because of the huge publicity gained for the organization through W. E. B. Dubois' editorship of the organization's The Crisis magazine, and through its legal expertise in court, particularly through its Legal Defense Fund (which became an independent civil rights organization in 1957).

J. The National Urban League. The National Urban League is one of the oldest, continuously operated non-governmental organizations in the USA. Formed officially in 1910 by combining two independent organizations—the New York-based Committee on Urban Conditions Among Negroes and the National League for the Protection of Colored Women—the NUL was originally named the National League on Urban Conditions Among Negroes, and adopted the shorter name, the National Urban League in 1920. The organization was formed as a response to the 1896 *Plessy v. Ferguson* case, which legalized Jim Crowism, and the resulting mass migrations of African Americans from the rural South to the North, Northwest, and West. In the many places Black folk settled, there was overt discrimination in employment, housing and educational facilities. To help African Americans find decent work and to fight employment discrimination, the NUL adopted a short-term and a long-term strategy of education and persuasion that included counseling, providing workshops, negotiating with businesses, and organizing protest marches when necessary "to enable African Americans to secure economic self-reliance, economic parity, power and civil rights." Its national leader in the early 1960s, Whitney M. Young, steered the organization into becoming a stalwart of the Civil Rights Movement. Though forbidden by its non-profit charter from openly engaging in mass political protests, the NUL became the primary host of several major planning meetings between A. Philip Randolph, Dr. Martin L. King, and other civil rights leaders involved in the famous March on Washington in 1963., and initiated such programs as the Street Academy, which was an alternative educational project for Black high school dropouts, and the New Thrust leadership training project to prepare youth activists for effective community-based problem solving. Currently, the NUL has over 100 local chapters located in 35 states and Washington, D.C. Choosing a strategy of semantic persuasion, the NUL has also published its "Opportunity Journal" since 1923, and annually, the NUL publishes the well-regarded national report, "State of Black America." Of the 10 presidents and executive directors of the NUL, the two most prominent have been Whitney Young and attorney Vernon Jordan.

K. The Congress of Racial Equality (CORE) (1942). The Congress of Racial Equality (CORE) was founded in 1942 by debater James Farmer, Bernice Fisher, and four other student-activists in Chicago. Its motto, based on Quaker principles and Buddhism, was "all people are created equal and should be committed towards achieving freedom and justice for all." CORE initiated the original "Freedom Rides" in 1947 by sending 16 of its male members on a two-week Journey of Reconciliation on Greyhound buses through Kentucky, North Carolina, and Virginia to challenge inter-state segregation in travel. In the early 1960s, as part of the youth initiatives during the Civil Rights Movement, CORE reinstituted that strategy and the Freedom Riders became a well-remembered component of the fight against Jim Crow. CORE also started the sit-ins against racial discrimination, and advocated the turn-the-other-cheek strategy, along with helping to organize the 1963 March on Washington. Working with SNCC (Student Non-violent Coordinating Committee) and the NAACP, CORE created the 1964 Freedom Summer project aimed at eradicating political and social discrimination against African Americans in the South. Out of this effort came Fannie Lou Hamer's Mississippi Freedom Democratic Party. Together, the three groups also established Freedom Schools throughout Mississippi, which garnered attendance from at least 3,000 youths, in the midst of firebombing, physical assaults and police harassment.

L. Mississippi Freedom Democratic Party (1964). Arguably, the single most important student-youth organization created during the 1960s in terms of its overall influence was the Student Non-Violent Coordinating Committee (SNCC). Formed in 1960 at the end of a civil rights youth conference organized by Ella Baker, the primary field organizer for Dr. King's and Rev. Joseph Lowery's Southern Christian Leadership Conference (SCLC). The conference was called at Shaw University in North Carolina to try and centralize youth efforts in the early days of the Civil Rights Movement, in the aftermath of the Greensboro and Nashville student sit-ins. Ella Baker helped to train SNCC's early members in consensus decision-making, rather than to allow top-down orders. Most SNCC decisions were made in long meetings in which anyone who had something to say on an issue, was allowed to say it until virtually everyone agreed with a particular course of action. Out of SNCC came the various wade-ins, march-ins and mass protests by youth during the Civil Rights era. SNCC workers were trained to live with and engage with the rural folk they were trying to organize to vote, to establish businesses, and to protest racial discrimination. Out of SNCC (along with CORE, the NAACP and other groups), came the Mississippi Freedom Democratic Party that challenged the all-white delegation to the 1964 Democratic National Convention; the creation of the Lowndes County Freedom Organization (Black Panther Party) Political Party in Alabama in 1965 (the first attempt to establish an all-Black alternative political party to register Blacks to vote and to run for elective office in the South—which was the forerunner of the California Black Panthers for Self-Defense organized by Huey Newton, Bobby Seale and others in California); the modern concept of Black Power (introduced by SNCC leaders Stokely Carmichael and Willie Ricks during the March Against Fear in Mississippi after James Meredith was shot); the thrust to create Black Studies departments in American colleges and universities; and the massive expansion of youth activism in the Civil Rights and Black Power Movements. The discussion of Black nationalism, Black community control over Black community resources, including land, the place of armed resistance in the struggle for freedom, all grew out of SNCC activism. By 1965, SNCC had the largest working staff of any civil rights organization and had coordinated direct action projects against segregated facilities and voter-education drives in Alabama, Arkansas, Maryland, Missouri, Louisiana, Kentucky, Tennessee, Illinois, North and South

Carolina, Mississippi and Georgia, had organized labor unions and two Black-independent political parties, agricultural cooperatives, advocated women's liberation, and other activities. SNCC did not create it, but clearly helped to usher in a new youth militancy and strategy of direct confrontation against racist power structures and activities.

M. Student Nonviolent Coordinating Committee (1960). National Black Political Convention, March, 1972. As one culmination of the youth militancy coming out of the recalcitrance of white racism seen again and again during the 1960s, and as an outgrowth of the Free Colored Convention Movement of the 19th century, a large number of activists who sought some tangible demonstration of political significance in the U.S.A. met in Gary, Indiana, hosted by Black mayor, Richard Hatcher. The gathering—a conclusion, of sorts, for the Black Power Movement—was memorable for the clashes of wills and the tenacity of political points of view, which finally all accumulated into a generally accepted National Black Political Agenda, which called for the election of a proportionate number of Black officials to represent Black communities all across the country, including election to Congress, Black community control of schools and other resources, a Black national health insurance program, etc. At that time, there was less than 500 Black elected officials throughout the U.S.A., including less than 10 in the U.S. government. By 2014, the number of Black elected officials had climbed to approximately 10, 950 out of over 550.000 elective posts. Thus the achievement of proportionate representation in Black elected officials had still not yet occurred. Also, the Black Political Agenda agreed upon in 1972 remains unfulfilled, as many of those elected have chosen not to focus on representing specifically Black American constituencies or their interests.

Chapter Eight

Political Factions and Political Parties

Distinctive to American democracy is the historical evolution of a two-party model of choosing political leadership. There are over 100 countries in the 21st century that claim and operate under some form of democratic governance. The U.S.A. is among only five (Spain, Jamaica, Malaysia, Portugal, and Australia being the others) that regularly operate through competitive elections and competitive administrations based on membership in one of two primary political parties. The vast majority of other democracies in the world are either one-party dominated, or multi-party operations. The American system allows numerous alternative parties, but those groups have historically been consigned to minority status because they have not won elections.

Additionally, the American party system emphasizes *candidate-centered* operations, that is, the political party brings candidates to the public based on candidates' perceived capacity to win election to office as measured by personal charisma and qualifications, not candidates' party loyalty or adherence to a specific political agenda.

Party-centered systems, as found in England and many other multi-party processes, emphasize candidate compliance with the party's agenda and platform, and candidates who try to launch independent views and actions contrary to party positions are generally disallowed from running for office again under that particular party banner. Party-centered systems allow much more discipline of party members than do candidate-centered systems.

In discussions of exporting American democracy to other countries, this two-party, candidate-centered version of an operating democracy, plus the idea of a dual democracy (republican and constitutional) is what is meant. However, it must be remembered that American democracy is a version tailored specifically for the historical experiences and conditions of existence in this country. American-style democracy is rather unique among world democracies and does not export well.

What Is a Political Party?

In general, in America:

A. A political party is a formal, legal entity registered in states as a corporation that can raise money and be sued.

B. A political party is a city-county-state-national organization with its own rules, procedures, discipline, structure, and methodologies for influencing the electorate and getting policy-makers into office and other positions of authority.

C. A political party is an organized body of volunteers and paid members who run candidates for president and vice president, Congress, state governor, state legislatures, and the like, and whose members are rewarded when their political party wins office. Parties have national political platforms, conventions, primaries, and caucuses. Political parties, as depicted by some commentators, are seen as essential to the maintenance and operations of democracies, since they perform vital functions, including

1. Managing, guiding and channeling the orderly transitions of political power and authority from one elected official to another;
2. Operating the principal vehicle for the public to choose rival candidates for office, including nominations (caucuses and primaries), campaigns, and elections;
3. Channeling public support for or public frustration with the government—essentially, acting as a direct link, a bridge, between government

and the community/constituency to hold government accountable for its obligations and promises;

4. Performing as a mediator and even broker for competing interests both within and outside the party ranks;

5. Operating the government as the party in power for the moment. Parties that win, appoint, and select most of the functionaries and staff, from presidential cabinet posts and federal judges to bureaucratic commissions and committee posts;

6. Recruiting qualified candidates for public office;

7. Unifying electorate constituencies consisting of ethnic diversities, different regional outlooks, conflicting ideologies and class orientations, etc., to participate in voting officeholders in and out of public leadership;

8. Providing an effective method of holding elected officials collectively accountable for the success or failure of their decisions and time in office.

Summarized Origins of American Political Parties

1) The first commonly recognized political party organized and designated in the American system was the Federalist Party of 1792, coordinated principally by Alexander Hamilton, George Washington's Secretary of State. However, while this was an actual, tangible grouping, it was an informal rather than formal political party, and some historians consider it as a political association or political club more than a distinct political party. That is, those associated with the Federalist Party were not "card-carrying" Federalists, but rather those who agreed mainly with Hamilton's positions and believed in a strong central government. The Federalists were an organized interest group unified around ideology and Washington's and Hamilton's personalities, and were a group that complied only partially with the definition of

American political parties noted above. Nonetheless, Hamilton did establish a network of supporters throughout the New England and Northeastern states, and the Federalists did successfully run candidates for national and state office, but there was no party structure, as such, and the ties to the party were mainly personal, rather than through structural or formal membership. The Federalists held the first national political party convention in 1795, re-elected George Washington as president in 1792, and elected John Adams as president in 1796.

2) As a foil to the fiscal and foreign policy directions advocated by Hamilton and his supporters in Congress and the president's cabinet, Thomas Jefferson, James Madison, and others of like minds formed an opposition coalition of farmers, states' rights champions, civil liberties advocates, and opposition to Great Britain that was eventually called Jeffersonian Republicans, Republican-Democrats, and finally just Democrats. This grouping is recognized by the modern Democratic Party as its parent political organization. However, similar to the Federalists, the Jeffersonian Republicans were an informal political association, rather than a formal political party from its 1793 inception through to the beginning of the 1820s.

3. The nascent Federalist Party faded principally over its lost credibility during the War of 1812. Spokesmen for the Federalists were accused of and roundly perceived as "traitors" because they advocated and tried to implement a separate peace treaty with England that then-President James Madison, did not authorize or support, and then Andrew Jackson's forces won the definitive Battle of New Orleans, which vanquished England militarily. In the absence of any real political opposition, the Democrat-Republicans won the White House from 1800 through 1824. The Republican-Democrats then split into two regionally oppositional groups, the other calling itself the National Republicans, and supporting banking, commerce, and manufacturing preferences, while the Jeffersonians still favored less big government and more rural interests, among other things.

4. Beginning in 1824, and becoming firmly established by 1828, the rural faction in this split, led by Andrew Jackson, created America's first modern political party, the Democrats. This group went far beyond being a mere political association or club, and was instead a national organization with state structures, patronage rules, and other aspects that complied with the definition provided above for political parties.

5. The loss of the election of 1832, again to Andrew Jackson and the Democrats, forced the National Republicans, as the other wing of the old Republican-Democrat grouping, to dissolve and to re-invent itself as a distinctive political party coalition named the Whig Party. This coalition became the dominant political party opposition to the Democrats from 1833 to 1856. The Whigs won the White House in 1840 and in 1848, but lost it again by 1852. That first election of 1840 won by the Whigs is recognized by most American political scientists as the decisive year and election that gave U.S. the first two modern political parties. Both the Democrats and Whigs held national conventions; both became legal entities; both fielded national and state candidates and campaigned in all sections of the country; both had local, state and national committees; both had primaries to select national candidates; and both produced national platforms.

6. In 1854, disaffected Whigs and abolitionists formed a brand new party around one major issue: destroying the American system of slavery. This was the beginning of the modern Republican Party, and it won its first presidential election with Abraham Lincoln in 1860, just before the start of the Civil War.

7. The Democrats and the Republicans have been America's two dominant political parties since 1856, and only once since the creation of the Republican Party has any presidential candidate come close to winning the White House without being either a member of the Democratic Party or the Republican Party. (That was in 1912 when Theodore Roosevelt, formerly the standard-bearer for the Republican Party who had already been a two-term president of the U.S.A., and had retired, created the Bull Moose Party after the Republicans refused to nominate him for another term. He won over 4 million popular votes, 27% of the total vote cast, and 88 electoral college votes as a Bull Mooser, which is still ranked as the strongest third-party performance in American political history.)

8. From the election of 1800 through the modern day, there have always been other political associations, and later legally recognized political parties, which have tried to challenge the two dominant parties, raise oppositional issues, act as election spoilers, and educate the public about

alternative voting preferences. These have included the Anti-Masonic Party, the Know-Nothings or American Party, the Socialist Party, the Peace and Freedom Party, the Progressive Party, the American Independent Party, the Libertarians, and many, many more. Collectively, they are referred to as American third parties, and they simply have not been successful, relatively speaking, in winning national or state elections.

Chapter Nine

Specific Powers of the Presidency

Primary presidential authority is contained in Article II of the U.S. Constitution and in a few scattered sentences in explanations contained in Articles I and III (for example, the president's veto powers). That statement seems definitive enough; however, since the 1788 ratification of the Constitution, the interpretation of the range and scope of that authority has been highly influenced by the vision or mindset of the fourty-four individuals—from 1789 to 2009—who have occupied the Oval Office, the make-up of Congress during each presidential administration, and the willingness of the Court majority to be either *strict constructionists* of the U.S. Constitution or *dynamic interpreters* of the document. The federal court, for example, has ruled on an accumulation of enhancements and limitations to presidential power and authority that collectively represents a "new" job description. This point will be explained in more detail below.

In its one-page, thirteen-paragraph portion of the Constitution, Article II focuses mainly on the necessary qualifications for office, succession to office in case of presidential incapacity or impeachment, the required electoral process for selecting a president every four years, and the oath of office. Article II utilizes only four of its paragraphs to specify presidential powers and authority, as it re-emphasizes that the president's primary function is to faithfully execute the laws passed by Congress, defend and execute the Constitution, and defend and protect America and its citizens. Clearly, the president has more authoritative clout than these four paragraphs indicate. From where does that extra authority derive? It comes from presidential claims of authority through the invisible Inherent Powers doctrine of the Constitution, and from Court interpretation.

First, in order to be elected president, one must be a "natural born" citizen who is at least 35 years old and who has lived in the United States for at least 14 years. "Natural born" has mainly been interpreted as *jus soli*, or born specifically on U.S. soil, although *jus sanguinis*, being born of American-citizen parents in a foreign land, also grants one automatic citizenship.

Second, the president is the chief executive officer of the U.S. government. As such, the president heads the executive branch of national government which currently consists of the president, the vice president (who also serves as president of the U.S. Senate), fifteen Cabinet Secretaries and their agencies, including the State Department, Defense Department, Treasury Department, Interior Department, Commerce Department, Health and Human Services Department, Transportation Department, Education Department, and over ten federal agencies, including the CIA, Homeland Security, NASA, the Office of Personnel Management (which alone handles over 2.8 million federal jobs), etc. It also includes the boards of directors for U.S. government-owned corporations such as Amtrak and the U.S. Post Office. The president appoints all fifteen of the Cabinet Secretaries (Cabinet Heads), and the U.S. Senate is authorized by the Constitution to hold hearings to ratify or disapprove of those presidential appointments. Though there is no specific constitutional language that identifies the appointing of presidential cabinet members, Article II, Section 2 of the Constitution states that the president may "require the Opinion, in writing, of the principal Officer in each of the executive Departments, upon any Subject relating to the Duties of their respective Offices." The interpretation of that constitutional excerpt has been used since George Washington's first term to allow the president to appoint a Cabinet of executive officers according to the number of Cabinet posts designated by Congress.

As the C.E.O. of U.S. government, the president is currently in specific charge of a federal bureaucracy that includes over 8,000 individual staff positions that the president must directly hire or approve of hiring (most of them listed in the *Plum Book*), over 587 federal judges (including the nine on the Supreme Court) whom the president has authority to appoint whenever vacancies occur, all U.S. ambassadors, ministers, and consuls to foreign countries, and other members of the diplomatic corps. Additionally, the president has a current staff of over 1,900 aides, assistants, advisors, and consultants to supervise.

Below is a list of presidential powers for which there is no significant dispute. Following that is a shorter list of designated powers and authority that has been variously interpreted and sometimes misunderstood through the years. Lastly, there is a list of powers the president does not have, and a look at the checks-and-balances process between Congress, the judiciary, and the president.

Distinct Powers and Authority of the U.S. President

The President:

1. Is the commander-in-chief of all U.S. armed forces, and commissions all officers of the U.S. government.
2. Grants clemency, which includes pardons, commutations, amnesties, and reprieves for convictions of any federal crime (any offenses against the U.S. except impeachment).
3. Convenes and adjourns special sessions of Congress when thought necessary.
4. Meets with and receives foreign ambassadors and dignitaries, and represents the U.S. internationally.
5. Appoints federal judges, ambassadors, envoys, and governmental representatives, with the advice and consent of the U.S. Senate.
6. Approves or vetoes (regular or pocket) all legislation passed by Congress.
7. Can issue executive orders to direct federal officials and agencies to act, and these become documents that have the force of law.
8. Can impound the federal budget (that is, freeze all federal government spending for a temporary period).
9. Can make recess appointments of federal officials and ambassadors while Congress is not in session.

10. Can negotiate binding treaties with foreign governments that then must be considered for ratification (confirmation) by two thirds of the U.S. Senate.

11. Can recognize new nations and new governments and negotiate "executive agreements" with foreign powers that are not subject to ratification by the U.S. Senate.

12. Can issue whatever orders are deemed necessary, including the authorization of military force, to protect Americans abroad, American property, and foreign nationals who are in the U.S.

13. Can propose, but cannot pass, legislation to Congress.

14. Can perform as the U.S. government's sole spokesperson for foreign affairs and can establish and conduct foreign affairs with or without congressional .consent.

15. Can perform as the sole negotiator of treaties with foreign entities, without congressional interference.

Presidential Powers Claimed but Disputed

1. Presidential emergency powers in times of national crisis (Lincoln seized extraordinary war powers that were declared unconstitutional by the Court, but he ignored that ruling; Truman tried to nationalize the nation's steel mills during a massive strike and the Court nullified his authority to do so; G. W. Bush arrested suspected terrorists without charging them and eavesdropped on Americans and had that authority limited by the Court, as examples).

2. Presidential executive privilege to withhold information from the public, Congress, and the federal Court on the basis of national security (Presidents from George Washington to G.W. Bush have used this authority and have been consistently challenged in doing so, as the Court has rebuffed Nixon in Watergate and Clinton in the Monica Lewinsky cases. There is no specific constitutional language that gives the authority of executive privilege to the president to withhold information. Washington's use of it gave the effort the status of a *privilege precedent* that successive presidents have relied upon as their rationale).

Expected Authority the President Does Not Have

1. The president does not have line-item veto authority. This is the authority to strike out or nullify, line-by-line if necessary, portions of congressional legislation, including the federal budget, which the president disagrees with. Virtually all state governors have this authority, but the president has to either approve or veto congressional legislation in its entirety. Congress tried to give this authority to President Bill Clinton in 1996, but the Supreme Court declared it unconstitutional.

2. The president does not have the authority to make the annual federal budget. In essence, the president annually presents to Congress a "wish list" of budgetary items and explanations. Congress, and Congress alone, legislates the federal budget.

3. The president cannot unilaterally nationalize American manufacturing entities (steel mills, railroads, etc.).

4. The president cannot officially declare the U.S. at war (although he can commit troops to protect American citizens and property without congressional authority).

5. The president cannot issue Executive Orders that are legally binding outside the scope of his constitutional powers and authority.

6. The president cannot refuse to comply with legal orders of Congress and/or the federal judiciary to produce documents necessary in investigations of criminal activity (although the issue of executive privilege in withholding information, related to this standard, remains in dispute and is regularly re-interpreted by the Court).

Important Court Cases That Have Refined the Authority of the President of the United States

1. *The Prize Cases* (1863): These cases—collectively the first of the five most significant cases refining the authority of the president—involved challenges regarding President Lincoln's authority to commit American troops against American states in rebellion. The ruling was that if the U.S. is attacked, either by a foreign entity or by American states in rebellion, the president has the complete authority to send

troops into combat to defend the country and protect American lives and property, whether war has been officially declared or not.

2. *Myers v. United States* (1926): This case—the second of the five most significant cases regarding presidential authority—determined that while the president alone had the vested power to remove Cabinet members and other subordinate federal executives, and this was enumerated power not inherent power, that presidential power was not unlimited.

3. *Humphrey's Executor v. United States* (1935): This case limited the power of the president to remove subordinate executives in positions explicitly created by Congress to only those specified reasons provided by Congress for removal.

4. *Morrison v. Olson* (1988): This case ruled that Congress can appoint a special prosecutor who can compel the attorney general and other executive officers to cooperate and comply with the special prosecutor's investigation.

5. *Youngstown Sheet and Tube Company v. Sawyer* (1952): This is another one of the five most significant cases in refining the authority of the president. The Court here declared unconstitutional a presidential executive order to nationalize the U.S. steel industry, to seize operational control of steel mills and plants, and to impose governmental directors. The E.O. was issued to kill a nationwide strike of steel workers thought to endanger the American public.

6. *United States v. Curtis-Wright Export Corp* (1936): This case, the fourth of the five most significant in this area, ruled that the president has the inherent power to establish and execute American foreign policy by his/her independent discretion.

7. *Nixon v. United States* (1974): This is the fifth of the five most significant cases in refining the authority of the president. The Court ruled that the president and the executive branch is required to respond cooperatively to requests for documents that are mandatory in an investigation of criminal conduct, and no claim of eexecutive privilege can undo such requirement.

8. *Clinton v. City of New York* (1998): This case declared unconstitutional the congressional granting of line-item veto authority to the president, as virtually all state governors have.

9. *Clinton v. Jones* (1997): This is a landmark case, held by a 9-0 Supreme Court ruling, that a sitting President of the United States has no immunity from civil law litigation against him for acts done before taking office as president and unrelated to the office of president.

Explaining A Myth: The President's Annual Budget

The yearly budget process in the U.S.A. is a complicated and cumbersome process. In summary, the president proposes a wish list of revenue and spending projects he (or she) *prefers, after taking into account the recommendations of Cabinet members, the budget director*, and other experts. That budget proposal is then submitted to Congress with or without a lot of public fanfare. It is Congress that formulates the annual budget, using the president's proposal as a reference point. Whether the president and the majority members of Congress are from the same political party or not, the president's proposals are always altered, adjusted, or dismissed. The president never gets all that he (or she) prefers, and there is a lot of political decision-making and deal-making that goes into every annual budget.

A Look at the Budgetary Process

1. The annual budget process traditionally begins in February and is supposed to be finished by October 1, the start of the government's fiscal year. However, the federal budget process now tends to run behind schedule, requiring the congressional passage of one or more "continuing resolutions" that keep the government operating until the real budget is finally authorized by congressional passage and presidential signature.

2. The budgetary process is a main ingredient in what is called the government's fiscal policy. The president's budgetary proposal informs Congress of the White House's vision for the three basic elements of U.S. fiscal policy: (1) how much money the government should spend on public needs and programs; (2) how much money the government should take in through taxes and other sources of revenue; and (3)

how large a deficit or surplus will result—simply the difference between money spent and money taken in.

3. After much haggling, debate, compromise, and adjustment regarding the president's proposal, Congress eventually hammers out its own version of the draft federal budget, called the budget resolution. Both the House and the Senate will come up with different versions of that document, which must then be merged together into a single piece of budgetary legislation. The eventual congressional budget resolution sets spending limits on discretionary government programs for the next five years as a yardstick to refer to every year.

4. The collective budget resolution will also authorize the programs targeted for government spending. Sometime after the budget resolution, the real meat-and-potatoes of the budgetary process takes place—the passage of a series of spending bills that will actually appropriate money to those programs. Authorization alone of a program in the budget is not enough. Congress has to approve the necessary appropriations or the program is not funded. Based on the Constitution, each spending bill must originate in the House of Representatives, which gives that branch enormous leverage in the budgetary process. Since the House and Senate versions of each spending bill must eventually be identical, this part of the process always becomes the most time-consuming ingredient in the budgetary process.

5. Once Congress has passed all of the annual spending bills (and there are always numbers of them) and submitted them to the president, the chief executive must either sign them into law or veto any of them (which means sending any rejected spending bills back to Congress for reconsideration and more haggling time). Should the spending bills sent to the president differ too much from what the president initially proposed (programs funded, spending levels appropriated, etc.), the veto pen is often put into operation. There is then more haggling, debate, and eventual compromise between the president's budgetary team and congressional staffers over each vetoed section. The president's signature on all the spending bills eventually agreed to by the president and Congress signals the end of the annual federal budget process (some spending bills never get signed).

Comparison Between Presidential Authority and That of the Governor of California

By contrast, looking at the fifteen specific powers listed in the previous section for the president, the governor of California has the formal authority to:

1. Make annual recommendations to the state legislature for future laws the governor prefers.
2. Approve or veto legislation within twelve days during regular sessions of the state legislature, and within thirty days when bills are submitted to the governor just before legislative recesses or adjournment (the bills otherwise become law without the governor's signature).
3. Submit the first draft of the state budget annually that already has in it the structure and fiscal relationships the governor wants. The governor thus has more influence initially over the state budget than the president has over the federal budget.
4. Make temporary appointments to some federal, state and county vacancies created by death or retirement of incumbents, including U.S. Senators, statewide elected officials and executive officers, county boards of supervisors, et al., until the next scheduled election for those positions. When it is a statewide elected official's position, both houses of the state legislature must approve the temporary appointment.
5. Make appointments to over 400 state boards and commissions, including, for example, the University of California Board of Regents, the Public Utilities Commission, the State Lottery Commission, the Water Resources Control Board, the Air Resources Board, and the State Lands Commission. These appointments require a majority vote of confirmation by the state senate.
6. Make appointments of over 2,650 state officials and judges (to the State Appeals Court and to the State Supreme Court). For the appointment of judges, the state legislature has no confirmation authority.
7. Call the legislature into special session to handle a specific state issue, like the budget.
8. Call special elections for important issues of the state.
9. Reorganize the entire state bureaucracy when deemed necessary.
10. Be the commander-in-chief of the California State National Guard

11. Issue pardons, reprieves, and commutations of criminal sentences
12. Make line-item veto changes in all monetary sections of bills submitted for the governor's signature, including fiscal changes in the state budget.However, the changes must be reductions or deletions of money appropriated, not increases, and this line-item authority extends only to the monetary part of legislation. All other legislation is either approved or vetoed as presented.
13. Issue executive orders within the range and scope of the governor's constitutional authority.

Although each state governor's authority is distinct, the vast majority hold authority similar to the California governor.

Presidential Actions that Have Affected the Inclusion Status of African Americans

The Emancipation Proclamation (1862, becoming law January 1, 1863) was issued by President Abraham Lincoln. It declared that all slaves in Confederate territory still in rebellion were thereby freed, although Mr. Lincoln did not, at the time, have executive authority in the southern states, and the proclamation freed virtually no one unless the Union Army was physically present to enforce it.

Executive Order 8802 (1942): Issued by President Franklin D. Roosevelt to ban racial discrimination in government departments and defense industries. It also created the Fair Employment Practices Committee to oversee compliance with the order.

Executive Order 9980 (1948): Issued by President Harry S. Truman, this law was aimed at promoting equal federal employment practices. "There shall be no discrimination in (federal personnel decisions) based on race, color, religion or national origin."

Executive Order 9981 (1948): Issued by President Harry S. Truman to integrate the U.S. armed forces.

Executive Order 10590 (1955): Issued by President Dwight D. Eisenhower to establish the President's Committee on Government Employment Policy. It was intended to eliminate discrimination in federal hiring policies and practices.

Executive Order 10925 (1961): Issued by President John F. Kennedy to establish the President's Committee on Equal Employment Opportunity, later to evolve into the Equal Employment Opportunity Commission. This required equal opportunity in placement and promotion in the U.S. military.

Executive Order 11063 (1962): Issued by President John F. Kennedy to ban segregation in federally funded housing.

Executive Order 11246 (1965): Issued by President Lyndon B. Johnson to prohibit discrimination in federal employment decisions on the basis of race, color, religion, sex, or national origin.

Executive Order 11478 (1969): Issued by President Richard M. Nixon to prohibit racial and ethnic discrimination in the competitive services of the federal civilian workforce, including the United States Postal Service and civilian employees of the United States Armed Forces.

Chapter Ten

Specific Powers of Congress

First, the specific powers and authority of Congress—the House of Representatives, as determined by proportionate or population-based representation and the U.S. Senate, based on each state getting two representatives—are articulated in seventeen paragraphs of Article I, Section 8 of the U.S. Constitution, as noted below and in Chapter 6. Additionally, Article IV, Section 3, and the XVI amendment (1913) provided several more specific powers of Congress.

Article I

Section 1. All legislative powers herein granted shall be vested in a Congress of the United States, which shall consist of a Senate and House of Representatives.

Section 2. The House of Representatives shall be composed of members chosen every second year by the people of the several states, and the electors in each state shall have the qualifications requisite for electors of the most numerous branch of the state legislature.

No person shall be a Representative who shall not have attained to the age of twenty five years, and been seven years a citizen of the United States, and who shall not, when elected, be an Inhabitant of that state In which he shall be chosen.

Representatives and direct taxes shall be apportioned among the several states that may be included within this union according to their respective numbers, which shall be determined by adding to the whole number of free persons, including those bound to service for a term of years and excluding Indians not taxed three-fifths of all other persons. The actual Enumeration shall be made within three years after the first meeting of the Congress of the United States, and within every subsequent term of ten years, in such manner as they shall by law direct. The number of Representatives shall not exceed one for every thirty thousand, but each state shall have at least one Representative; and until such enumeration shall be made, the state of New Hampshire shall be entitled to choose three, Massachusetts eight, Rhode Island and Providence Plantations one, Connecticut five, New York six, New Jersey four, Pennsylvania eight, Delaware one, Maryland six, Virginia ten, North Carolina five, South Carolina five, and Georgia three.

When vacancies happen in the Representation from any state, the executive authority thereof shall issue writs of election to fill such vacancies.

The House of Representatives shall choose their speaker and other officers; and shall have the sole power of impeachment.

Section 3. The Senate of the United States shall be composed of two Senators from each state, chosen by the legislature thereof, for six years; and each Senator shall have one vote.

Immediately after they shall be assembled in consequence of the first election. They shall be divided as equally as may be into three classes. The seats of the Senators of the first class shall be vacated at the expiration of the second year of the second class at the expiration of the fourth year and the third class at the expiration of the sixth year so that one third may be chosen every second year; and if vacancies happen by resignation or otherwise during the recess of the legislature of any state, the executive thereof may make temporary appointments until the next meeting of the legislature, which shall then fill such vacancies.

No person shall be a Senator who shall not have attained to the age of thirty years, and been nine years a citizen of the United States and who shall not, when elected, be an inhabitant of that state for which be shall be chosen.

The Vice President of the United States shall be President of the Senate, but shall have no vote, unless they be equally divided.

The Senate shall choose their other officers, and also a President pro tempore, In the absence of the Vice President, or when he shall exercise the office of President of the United States.

The Senate shall have the sole power to try all impeachments. When sitting for that purpose, they shall be on oath or affirmation. When the President of the United States is tried, the Chief Justice shall preside: And no person shall be convicted without the concurrence of two thirds of the members present.

Judgment in cases of impeachment shall not extend further than to removal from office, and disqualification to hold and enjoy any office of honor, trust or profit under the United States: but the party convicted shall nevertheless be liable and subject to indictment, trial, judgment and punishment, according to law.

Section 4. The times, places and manner of holding elections for Senators and Representatives, shall be prescribed in each state by the legislature thereof; but the Congress may at any time by law make or alter such regulations, except as to the places of choosing Senators.

The Congress shall assemble at least once in every year, and such meeting shall be on the first Monday in December. unless they shall by law appoint a different day.

Section 5. Each House shall be the judge of the elections, returns and qualifications of its own members, and a majority of each shall constitute a quorum to do business; but a smaller number may adjourn from day to day, and may be authorized to compel the attendance of absent members, in such manner, and under such penalties as each House may provide. Each House may determine the rules of its proceedings, punish its members for disorderly behavior, and, with the concurrence of two thirds, expel a member.

Each House shall keep a journal of its proceedings, and from time to time publish the same, excepting such parts as may in their judgment require secrecy; and the yeas and nays of the members of either House on any question shall, at the desire of one fifth of those present, be entered on the journal.

Neither House, during the session of Congress, shall, without the consent of the other, adjourn for more than three days, nor to any other place than that in which the two Houses shall be sitting.

Section 6. The Senators and Representatives shall receive a compensation for their services, to be ascertained by law, and paid out of the treasury of the United States. They shall in all cases, except treason, felony and breach of the peace, be privileged from arrest during their attendance at the session of their respective Houses, and in going to and returning from the same; and for any speech or debate in either House, they shall not be questioned in any other place.

No Senator or Representative shall, during the time for which he was elected, be appointed to any civil office under the authority of the United States, which shall have been created, or the emoluments whereof shall have been increased during such time: and no person holding any office under the United States, shall be a member of either House during his continuance in office.

Section 7. All bills for raising revenue shall originate in the House of Representatives; but the Senate may propose or concur with amendments as on other Bills.

Every bill which shall have passed the House of Representatives and the senate, shall, before it become a law, be presented to the President of the United States; if he approve he shall sign it, but if not he shall return it, with his objections to that House in which it shall have originated, who shall enter the objections at large on their journal, and proceed to reconsider it. If after such reconsideration two thirds of that House shall agree to pass the bill, it shall be sent, together with the objections, to the other House, by which it shall likewise be reconsidered, and if approved by two thirds of that House, it shall become a law. But in all such cases the votes of both Houses shall be determined by yeas and nays, and the names of the persons voting for and against the bill shall be entered on the journal of each House respectively. If any bill shall not be returned by the President within ten days (Sundays excepted) after it shall have been presented to him, the same shall be a law, in like manner as if he had signed it, unless the Congress by their adjournment prevent its return, in which case it shall not be a law.

Every order, resolution, or vote to which the concurrence of the Senate and House of Representatives may be necessary (except on a question of adjournment) shall be presented to the President of the United States; and before the same shall take effect, shall be approved by him, or being disapproved by him, shall be repassed by two thirds of the Senate and House of Representatives, according to the rules and limitations prescribed in the case of a bill.

Section 8. The Congress shall have power to lay and collect taxes, duties, imposts and excises, to pay the debts and provide for the common defense and general welfare of the United States; but all duties, imposts and excises shall be uniform throughout the United States;

To borrow money on the credit of the United States;

To regulate commerce with foreign nations, and among the several states, and with the Indian tribes;

To establish a uniform rule of naturalization, and uniform laws on the subject of bankruptcies throughout the United States;

To coin money, regulate the value thereof, and of foreign coin, and fix the standard of weights and measures;

To provide for the punishment of counterfeiting the securities and current coin of the United States;

To establish post offices and post roads;

To promote the progress of science and useful arts, by securing for limited times to authors and inventors the exclusive right to their respective writings and discoveries;

To constitute tribunals inferior to the Supreme Court;

To define and punish piracies and felonies committed on the high seas, and offenses against the law of nations;

To declare war, grant letters of marque and reprisal, and make rules concerning captures on land and water;

To raise and support armies, but no appropriation of money to that use shall be for a longer term than two years;

To provide and maintain a navy;

To make rules for the government and regulation of the land and naval forces;

To provide for calling forth the militia to execute the laws of the union, suppress insurrections and repel invasions;

To provide for organizing, arming, and disciplining, the militia, and for governing such part of them as may be employed in the service of the United States, reserving to the states respectively, the appointment of the officers, and the authority of training the militia according to the discipline prescribed by Congress;

To exercise exclusive legislation in all cases whatsoever, over such District (not exceeding ten miles square) as may, by cession of particular states, and the acceptance of Congress, become the seat of the government of the United States, and to exercise like authority over all places purchased by the consent of the legislature of the state In which the same shall be, for the erection of forts, magazines, arsenals, dockyards, and other needful buildings;—And

To make all laws which shall be necessary and proper for carrying into execution the foregoing powers, and all other powers vested by this Constitution In the government of the United States, or in any department or officer thereof.

Section 9. The migration or importation of such persons as any of the states now existing shall think proper to admit, shall not be prohibited by the Congress prior to the year one thousand eight hundred and eight, but a tax or duty may be imposed on such importation, not exceeding ten dollars for each person.

The privilege of the writ of habeas corpus shall not be suspended, unless when in cases of rebellion or invasion the public safety may require it.

No bill of attainder or ex post facto law shall be passed.

No capitation or other direct tax shall be laid unless in proportion to the census or enumeration herein before directed to be taken.

No tax or duty shall be laid on articles exported from any state. No preference shall be given by any regulation of commerce or revenue to the ports of one state over those of another: nor shall vessels bound to, or from, one state, be obliged to enter, clear or pay duties in another.

No money shall be drawn from the treasury, but in consequence of appropriations made by law; and a regular statement and account of receipts and expenditures of all public money shall be published from time to time.

No title of nobility shall be granted by the United States: and no person holding any office of profit or trust under them, shall, without the consent of the Congress, accept of any present, emolument, office, or title, of any kind whatever, from any king, prince, or foreign state.

Section 10. No state shall enter into any treaty, alliance, or confederation; grant letters of marque and reprisal; coin money; emit bills of credit; make anything but gold and silver coin a tender in payment of debts; pass any bill of attainder, ex post facto law, or law impairing the obligation of contracts, or grant any title of nobility.

No state shall, without the consent of the Congress, lay any imposts or duties on Imports or exports, except what may be absolutely necessary for executing its inspection laws: and the net produce of all duties and Imposts, laid by any state on imports or exports, shall be for the use of the treasury of the United States; and all such laws shall be subject to the revision and control of the Congress.

No state shall, without the consent of Congress, lay any duty of tonnage, keep troops, or ships of war in time of peace, enter into any agreement or compact with another state, or with a foreign power, or engage in war, unless actually invaded, or in such imminent danger as will not admit of delay.

Article IV, Section 3
New States may be admitted by the Congress into this Union; but no new State shall be formed or erected within the Jurisdiction of any other State; nor any State be formed by the Junction of two or more States, or Parts of States, without the Consent of the Legislatures of the States concerned as well as of the Congress.

The Congress shall have Power to dispose of and make all needful Rules and Regulations respecting the Territory or other Property belonging to the United States; and nothing in this Constitution shall be so construed as to Prejudice any Claims of the United States, or of any particular State.

Amendment XVI (Ratified February 3, 1913.)
The Congress shall have power to lay and collect taxes on incomes, from whatever source derived, without apportionment among the several States, and without regard to any census or enumeration.

Even in the old English of the 18th century, the words, descriptions and prescriptions laying out what Congress could and could not do in the U.S. government seemed specific and clear. These are the *enumerated powers* and authority of Congress as the legislative branch of the federal government.

However clear and specific the language seems, nonetheless, exactly how to implement, operate and enforce those congressional powers and authority has been the continuing subject of court challenges and interpretation since the Constitution was ratified in 1788. Thus, there are both the specific, constitutionally enumerated powers of Congress, and also the "resulting" powers of Congress that are even greater and more limited based on federal court interpretations. For example, only Congress has the "necessary and proper clause" authority to create whatever laws it deems necessary, according to *Maryland v. McCulloch,* 1819.

These "resulting powers" of Congress include:

1. The power of Congress to delegate its authority to numerous boards, commissions and other entities in order to get government work done (e.g., Congress created the Interstate Commerce Commission to regulate the rates and practices of railroads with respect to interstate commerce; the Federal Communications Commission to license broadcasting stations and to exert exclusive jurisdiction and authority over the media and communications industry; and the Sentencing Commission, an independent agency in the judicial branch of government, to develop and promulgate guidelines binding federal judges and restricting their discretion in sentencing criminal defendants in federal cases.)

2. The power to participate in acquiring territory for the U.S. either by treaty, discovery or conquest and the right to establish rules for governing that territory.

3. The power to declare the quality of paper to be used and the value given to all U.S. currency.

4. The power to declare the payment of all legal debts in the U.S. currency Congress designates

5. The power to legislate for all Indian tribes living within the U.S.

6. The power to exclude, arrest and deport all undesirable immigrants

7. The power to require all immigrants and non-citizens to register and be fingerprinted.

8. The power to maintain the complete sovereignty of the U.S. government in its conduct of foreign affairs.

9. The power to tax and raise revenue (thus, the Department of Internal Revenue)

10. The power to admit states into the United States.

As articulated and interpreted by federal court rulings and customary practice, congressional authority and power, which currently falls into three categories (*Specifically Delegated or Enumerated, Implied,* and *Special Powers*) is summarized in the listing here:

A. The categories of Delegated or Enumerated powers of Congress are Fiscal and Monetary Powers to be used to pay our country's debts and to provide for the defense and well-being of the country as a whole. Congress is also responsible for levying and collecting taxes from citizens and businesses to fund national governmental operations. Congress controls the borrowing of money for the U.S. and the coining and printing of the U.S. currency. Congress also establishes standards for weights and measures (America still uses feet, inches, and pounds, for example, rather than the metric system) and punishes counterfeiters.

1. Trade Regulation

Congress regulates both foreign trade and commerce between American states. However, Congress is prohibited from passing legislation that gives a clear advantage in trade between one state and another in the U.S.

2. Military Power

Congress is responsible for establishing and maintaining a national military force, including the organization and enforcement of military laws. Only Congress has the power to declare war.

3. Additional Specific Powers:

Congress establishes rules for citizenship in the United States, maintains a national post office system, makes laws for copyrights and patents, and governs the District of Columbia. Only Congress has the constitutional power to establish our federal court system (see the Judiciary Act, 1789).

B. Examples of the implied powers of Congress (mainly under the necessary and proper clause) include:

1. Imposing Spending Power Restrictions on States

In the 1987 case of *South Dakota v. Dole,* the Supreme Court considered a federal law that required the Secretary of Transportation to withhold 5% of a state's federal highway dollars if the state allowed persons less than 21 years of age to purchase alcoholic beverages. South Dakota, which allowed 18-year-olds to drink and stood to lose federal funds for highway construction, sued the Secretary of Transportation, arguing that the law was not a constitutional exercise of the power of Congress to spend, but rather was an attempt to enact a national drinking age. In upholding the federal law, the Court announced a four-part test for evaluating the constitutionality of conditions attached to federal spending programs: (1) the spending power must be exercised in pursuit of the general welfare, (2) grant conditions must be clearly stated, (3) the conditions must be related to a federal interest in the national program or project, and (4) the spending power cannot be used to induce states to do things that would themselves be unconstitutional. The Court interpreted the grant condition to be a financial "inducement" for South Dakota to enact a higher drinking age rather than financial "compulsion" to do so. In dissent, Justice O'Connor argued that spending conditions should be found constitutional only if they related to how the federal grant dollars were to be spent.

2. Legislating Power and Property Regulations
In 1976, a dispute over nineteen wild burros rounded up on federal land and sold by New Mexico's Livestock Board reached the Supreme Court (*New Mexico v. Kleppe*). The Department of Interior argued that New Mexico's action violated the Wild Free-Roaming Horses and Burros Act, while New Mexico countered that the Act exceeded the power granted to Congress by the Property Clause of Article IV, Section 3. New Mexico contended that Congress could regulate only those state actions on federal land that threaten to damage public lands. The Court rejected this narrow interpretation. Congress has the power to enact "needful" regulations "respecting" the public lands and the Court decided that a "needful" regulation is a decision "entrusted primarily to the judgment of Congress." The Court concluded the federal government "has a power over its own property analogous to the police power" of the states.

Selected Acts of Congress that Specifically Affected the Status of Black Americans

- The Ordinance of 1787: The Northwest Territorial Government ("Northwest Ordinance"), the first congressional legislation that dealt with slavery as a national issue by restricting its expansion beyond the Ohio River.

- Fugitive Slave Law of 1793, a states-rights-oriented act that legalized slave-catching activities between states in order to protect slave owners.
- An Act to prohibit the importation of slaves 1807. This is the American legislation that officially ends this country's participation in the transatlantic slave trade. It says nothing, however, about the domestic American slave trade.
- Fugitive Slave Law of 1850: The most stringent fugitive slave act ever passed. It required compliance by imposing a fine of up to $1,000 on federal marshals or other officials who did not arrest an alleged runaway slave brought to their attention. It also made free Blacks liable to be immediately reduced to slavery.
- The Missouri Compromise (1850) was a series of Congressional legislative measures addressing slavery, the admission of territories into American statehood, and the boundaries of territories acquired during the Mexican-American War (1846–1848).
- The Kansas-Nebraska Act (1854) created the states of Kansas and Nebraska, and gave territories that wanted to become states the authority to have "popular sovereignty," or a citizen's vote to determine whether to enter as a slave or non-slave state. This caused a virtual civil war in Kansas between the slave-holding and non-slave-holding interests.
- The Enrollment Act (Conscription) was America's first draft law and required all male citizens in the North to register as conscripts for the war. In New York, there was a massive riot as a result, in which mainly working class Irish attacked anyone thought to be Black. There was a devastating loss of life and property among African Americans in New York City, and martial law had to be temporarily imposed. At the time, this was the worst riot in American history.
- Civil Rights Act of 1866. Declared that all persons born in the United States were citizens, without regard to race, color, or previous condition of servitude.
- Bureau of Refugees, Freedmen and Abandoned Lands (1865 and 1866). This act created the first federal bureau to distribute food and land, to provide schools, healthcare, and military protection to ex-slaves. President Andrew Johnson tried to veto the act in 1866, but Congress overrode it.

- Reconstruction Act. A series of four interconnected legislative acts aimed at organizing the division of all former Confederate states into five military districts under martial law. Each district would be headed by a military commander who was charged with ensuring that the states would create new constitutions and eventually ratify the Fourteenth Amendment in order to be re-entered into the U.S. in good standing.
- Southern Homestead Act of 1866. Passed on July 21, 1866, the Southern Homestead Act opened up 46 million acres (190,000 km²) of federal public land for sale at discounted prices in Alabama, Arkansas, Florida, Louisiana, and Mississippi primarily for poverty-stricken Southerners, Black and White, in 160-acre plots. The primary beneficiaries for the first six months were freedmen, but the law was repealed in 1876 before much land was distributed to them.
- Naturalization Act of 1870: This was an anti-Asian legislative act that defined persons eligible for American citizenship as only "white persons and persons of African descent," deliberately excluding Asians and others.
- Enforcement Act of 1870, of 31 May 1870.
- Enforcement Act of 1871, of February 1871.
- Enforcement Act of 1871: Also known as the Ku Klux Klan Enforcement Act. It was the third enforcement act passed by Congress. The act gave the United States president the power to suspend the writ of habeas corpus to combat the Ku Klux Klan and other White terrorist organizations during the Reconstruction Era.
- Amnesty Act (1872). This legislation pardoned over 150,000 former Confederate soldiers (not in officer or leadership positions during the war) and helped to usher in the end of Reconstruction and Black progress during that period. Most of these became Southern Democrats who tried to vote out Reconstruction laws, but Black Republicans consistently outvoted them until 1877.
- Morrill Land Grant Colleges Act (1890). This legislation created the Historically Black Colleges and Universities in America. The legislation required each state to show that race was not an admissions criterion for its higher education institutions, or else to build separate land-grant institutions for persons of color.
- Civil Rights Act of 1957.

- Civil Rights Act of 1960.
- Civil Rights Act of 1964.
- Economic Opportunity Act of 1964.
- Voting Rights Act of 1965.
- Civil Rights Act of 1968.
- Civil Rights Act of 1982.
- Civil Rights Act of 1991.

The African American drive for civil rights and civil liberties through the years has mainly focused on equal access to voting, equal opportunity in employment, affirmative action in education, and achieving prohibitions against certain forms of "categorical discrimination." Categorical discrimination includes exclusions based on race, gender, or disability, from public education, employment, housing, and public accommodations.

African Americans in the U.S. Congress

In 2013, in the 112th Congress, counting the recent election of New Jersey's Corey Booker, there are forty-four African Americans collectively serving in the House and Senate, with one appointed Senator (Mo Cowan) scheduled to be "retired" after a September Special Election in Massachusetts for a "permanent" replacement for new Secretary of State John Kerry, the long-time senator for that state. Starting in 1870 during Reconstruction, to date there have been 136 African American members of Congress, including 127 members of the House of Representatives, and nine U.S. Senators, six of whom were elected. Of that number, there have been 106 Democrats, including 101 in the House and five in the Senate; and thirty Republicans, including twenty-six in the House and four in the U.S. Senate. Those 136 members have represented twenty-seven states. (See Figure 1-A)

During Reconstruction, there were fifteen African Americans, all Republicans, elected to Congress, with Hiram Revels being recorded as the first African American elected to Congress. (See Figure 2-A) The last African American elected during that time period was out of office by 1901, and there was not another African American elected until twenty-eight years later (Oscar DePriest, Illinois). Since then (1929), there has been a steady Black American presence in Congress (all in the House until 1967). The last Reconstruction Senator—Blanche K. Bruce, from Mississippi—was out of office in 1881, and there was not another African American elected to the Senate for nearly 100 years, until Edward Brooke of Massachusetts was elected to two full Senate terms starting in 1967. Arthur Mitchell, representing Illinois, was the first African American Democrat elected to Congress, and was so elected in 1935 and served until 1943.

States That Elected African American Congresspersons (Figure 1.A)

Alabama (6)

California (12)

Connecticut (1)

Florida (7)

Georgia (8)

Illinois (17-3 Senators)

Indiana (3)

Louisiana (4)

Maryland (5)

Massachusetts (1)

Michigan (6)

Minnesota (1)

Mississippi (5)

Missouri (4)

New Jersey (3)

New York (9)

North Carolina (8)

Ohio (3)

Oklahoma (1)

Pennsylvania (4)

South Carolina (10)

Tennessee (2)

Texas (6)

Virginia (2)

Wisconsin (1)

African American Congresspersons During and Just After Reconstruction (Figure 2.A)

NAME	STATE REPRESENTED	POSITION	YEARS IN OFFICE
Blanche K. Bruce	Mississippi	Senator	1875–1881
Richard Cain	South Carolina	H.R.	1873–1875, 77–79
Henry Cheatham	North Carolina	H.R.	1889–1893
Robert Delarge	South Carolina	H.R.	1871–1873
Robert Elliot	South Carolina	H.R.	1871–1874

Jeremiah Haralson	Alabama	H.R.	1875–1877
John Hyman	North Carolina	H.R.	1875–1877
Jefferson Long	Georgia	H.R.	1871–1873
John M. Langston	Virginia	H.R.	1890–1891
John Lynch	Mississippi	H.R.	1873–77, 1882–83
Thomas E. Miller	South Carolina	H.R.	1889–1891
George Murray	South Carolina	H.R.	1893–1897
Charles Nash	Louisiana	H.R.	1875–1877
James O'Hara	North Carolina	H.R.	1883–1887
Hiram Revels	Mississippi	Senator	1870–71
Joseph Rainey	South Carolina	H.R.	1870–1879
Alonzo Ransier	South Carolina	H.R.	1873–1875
James Rapier	Alabama	H.R.	1873–1875
Robert Smalls	South Carolina	H.R.	1875–79, 1882–87
Benjamin Turner	Alabama	H.R.	1871–1873
Josiah Walls	Florida	H.R.	1871–1876
George White	North Carolina	H.R.	1897–1901

Chapter Eleven

The American Judiciary

The American judiciary, also called the judicial branch of government, is a hierarchy of levels of courts in the country headed by the U.S. Supreme Court. The Supreme Court exists as the only specific court created by the U.S . Constitution. That designation is in Article III.

Congress, which has the power to decide on the number of justices who serve on the Supreme Court (the number has gone from six to ten previously to nine currently), also has the constitutional power to establish all the other courts under the Supreme Court. Thus, Congress has created thirteen federal courts of appeals and ninety-five federal district courts. The U.S. president has the authority to appoint all federal judges (there are currently 587 of them in total) as vacancies occur, including justices of the Supreme Court, with the advice and consent of the U.S. Senate. The Supreme Court holds its judicial sessions in Washington, D.C., and the other federal courts are located in various cities throughout the United States.

Basic Facts About the Judiciary

1. Congress created the current American court system with the passage of the Judiciary Act of 1789. That, along with several later additions to the act, created all the levels of courts under the Supreme Court.

2. Federal justices, including those on the Supreme Court, are appointed by the president, and must be confirmed by majority vote of the U.S. Senate (the current interpretation of the constitutional provision for the Senate "to advise and consent"). Once confirmed, these are lifetime appointments vacated only by retirements, resignation, death, or congressional impeachment.

3. The Constitution establishes no qualifications for Supreme Court justices, which means one does not have to be an attorney with prior bench experience, or a former judge on a lower court. Current procedures and prior practice generally call for nominations of individuals by the president based on a nominee's legal experience, competence, demonstrated ethics, political affiliation, and the results of public interviews with the Senate.

4. The Chief Justice of the Supreme Court is actually the Chief Justice of the United States Court System and is the head of the judicial branch of America. The other eight justices are Associate Justices of the United States Supreme Court. The Chief Justice assigns the writing of opinions to the other justices, and it is the Chief Justice who presides at impeachment trials coordinated by the U.S. Senate.

5. The Supreme Court has two kinds of jurisdiction: original jurisdiction (i.e., cases that begin and end in the Supreme Court), and *final appeal jurisdiction*, i.e., for cases already decided at lower courts. For original jurisdiction, the Supreme Court handles cases in which the major issues are:

   a. The U.S. Constitution, federal laws, treaties with foreign nations, and maritime affairs

   b. Matters concerning U.S. ambassadors, ministers, or consuls

   c. Cases in which the U.S. government or a state government is a party

   d. Disputes between states and cases otherwise involving interstate (or state-to-state) relations

e. Final appeal trials, the Supreme Court chooses up to one hundred cases a year through its *writ of certiorari-process.* There is no mandatory right of appeal to the Supreme Court.

6. The Judiciary Act divided the United States into a federal court system that included twelve (now thirteen) judicial districts or *judicial circuits.* The ninety-four geographical districts under those circuits are in the eastern, central, southern and western areas of the country, and within each of those is one court of appeals, a regional district court, and a series of U.S. bankruptcy courts.

7. The only federal court that can issue interpretations of federal law that bind state courts is the Supreme Court itself. Decisions of the lower federal courts on issues of federal law are persuasive rulings but not binding authority in the states in which those federal courts sit.

8. The official policy-making body for the U.S. court system is called the Judicial Conference of the United States. It monitors, adjusts, creates, and otherwise revises rules of federal judicial procedure. Additionally, the U.S. Marshals Service provides protection for the federal judges, and for transporting federal prisoners.

9. In the federal court system, it is the U.S. District Courts that serve as the federal trial courts. On occasion, these courts will hear appeals from a lower, specialized court, but in general, federal court cases start in the U.S. District Courts. The intermediate courts, operating under a system of mandatory review or appeal from the lower courts, are the U.S.. Courts of Appeal. They must hear all referred cases from the U.S. District Courts. The Supreme Court has discretionary review , which means it can choose which cases it will hear under review, and which cases it won't.

10. Judicial independence theoretically arises for federal judges in that neither Congress, nor any other agency of the government, can reduce the salary of a sitting judge, and, once confirmed, federal judges are appointed for life.

Separate from, but not entirely independent of, this federal court system are the individual court systems of each state, each dealing with its own laws and having its own court rules and procedures.

The supreme court of each state is the final authority on the interpretation of that state's laws and constitution. A case may be appealed from a state court to the U.S. Supreme Court only if there is a federal question (an issue arising under the U.S. Constitution, or laws/treaties of the United States). The relationship between federal and state laws is extremely complex and confusing as a result of the unique nature of American federalism. For example, a state supreme court is bound *only* by the U.S. Supreme Court's interpretation of federal law, but is *not* bound by interpretation of federal law by the federal court of appeals for the circuit in which the state sits, or even the federal district courts located in the state. Conversely, a federal district court hearing a matter involving only a question of state law (usually through diversity jurisdiction) must apply the substantive law of the state in which the court sits, as if the federal court were a court of that state (but at the same time, the case is heard under the Federal Rules of Civil Procedure instead of local rules, which may be quite different). Together the laws of the federal and state governments form U.S. law.

Especially after the 19th century, the African American fight for inclU. usion has focused on direct action and judicial pursuits, with congressional legislation as a secondary strategy.

The California Court System

Although California citizens deal most frequently with their municipal court for traffic tickets and many other adventures, the bulk of the California State court system is organized around three interrelated levels of judicial activities: the Superior Court, the State Court of Appeal, and the California State Supreme Court. All three levels handle both civil and criminal matters, with the Superior Court functioning as the primary trial court of the state. There is at least one Superior Court in each of California's 58 counties, and 6 Appeal Court Districts (1st District—San Francisco, 2nd District—Los Angeles and Ventura, 3rd District—Sacramento, 4th District—San Diego and San Bernardino, 5th District—Fresno, and 6th District—San Jose). The system also includes the Small Claims Courts for civil matters in dispute at or below $7,500.

Maintaining and monitoring the court system are four state bureaus: (1)the Commission on Judicial Appointments (primarily for Supreme

Court and Courts of Appeal recommendations); (2) the Commission on Judicial Nominees (focusing on the Superior Court); (3) the Commission on Judicial Performance; and (4) the Judicial Council (to administer the system).

Judges are elected, appointed, and the Supreme Court and Courts of Appeal justices are subject to citizen approval or rejection by referendum every twelve years. Removal of a judge in California is through one of four approaches:

1. Through citizens voting to elect someone else.
2. Impeachment, conviction, and removal by the State Legislature.
3. Recall through a ballot initiative based on 20% of registered voters.
4. Recommended for removal by the Commission on Judicial Performance after conviction of a felony, or conviction of moral turpitude.

Currently, the California state court system has over 1,600 judges and 19,000 court employees.

Chapter Twelve

Elections

The President of the U.S. Is Selected by the Electoral College

Although American citizens who are registered voters in a state jurisdiction cast a ballot for a presidential nominee on election day (the first Tuesday in November), every four years, in reality they are electing "electors," who are people pre-selected by each political party with a candidate in the race, and it is those people who will cast the deciding ballots for the presidency. This is what is called the Electoral College, and it is a non-direct election device created by the signers of the U.S. Constitution, most of whom distrU.S.ted direct democracy in the hands of everyday citizens. Every four years, there is talk of getting rid of this clunky approach, but it remains and will remain a part of the American system. It will take a constitutional amendment to either get rid of it or radically alter it and the political will to do either has not been forthcoming. Meanwhile, electoral votes by these "electors," who, by the way, are selected for their party loyalty, but who sometimes have not followed the script when their ballots are cast, are based on congressional representation—the sum of senators and representatives.

There is consistent scuttlebutt bandied about every four years that because of this electoral college device, the votes of ordinary citizens do not count. Quite the contrary. It is the cumulative votes of regular citizens—the popular vote—that determines the votes of the "electors" in each state.

Although not bound by law to do so, virtually every "elector" for the last half century or so has voted the way the popular vote came out. Public and party pressures, and a consistent party system of reward and punishment, have cumulatively become an effective method of keeping "electors" on the straight and narrow.

Electoral votes are from the congressional representation from each state, based on the total number of U.S. senators and members of the House of Representatives. The total in Congress is 538 and 270 electoral votes (simple majority) are needed to be elected president. Below is each state's past and current (2000 to 2010) electoral vote count. Changes in the electoral vote count reflect increases or decreases in that state's population.

Total Electoral Votes: 538; Majority Needed to Elect: 270

State	
Alabama	9—9
Alaska	3—3
Arizona	8—11
Arkansas	6—6
California	54—55
Colorado	8—9
Connecticut	8—7
Delaware	3—3
District of Columbia	3—3
Florida	25—29
Georgia	13—16
Hawaii	4—4
Idaho	4—4
Illinois	22—20
Indiana	12—11
Iowa	7—6
Kansas	6—6
Kentucky	8—8
Louisiana	9—8
Maine	4—4
Maryland	10—10
Massachusetts	12—11
Michigan	18—16
Minnesota	10—10
Mississippi	7—6
Missouri	11—10
Montana	3—3
Nebraska	5—5

Nevada	5—6
New Hampshire	4—4
New Jersey	15—14
New Mexico	5—5
New York	31—29
North Carolina	15—15
North Dakota	3—3
Ohio	20—18
Oklahoma	8—7
Oregon	7—7
Pennsylvania	21—20
Rhode Island	4—4
South Carolina	8—9
South Dakota	3—3
Tennessee	11—11
Texas	34—38
Utah	5—6
Vermont	3—3
Virginia	13—13
Washington	11—12
West Virginia	5—5
Wisconsin	11—10
Wyoming	3—3

Source: U.S. Census Bureau ,Last Update: 12/10/2010

Electoral College: A Little Background

From the Constitution: Article II, Section I:

Clause 2. Each State shall appoint, in such Manner as the Legislature thereof may direct, a Number of Electors, equal to the whole Number of Senators and Representatives to which the State may be entitled in the Congress; but no Senator or Representative, or Person holding an Office of Trust or Profit under the United States, shall be appointed an Elector.

Clause 3. The Electors shall meet in their respective States and vote by Ballot for two Persons, of whom one at least shall not be an Inhabitant of the same State with themselves. And they shall make a List of all the Persons voted for, and of the Number of Votes for each, which List they shall sign and certify, and transmit sealed to the Seat of Government of the United States, directed to the President of the Senate .The President of the Senate shall, in the presence of the Senate and House of Representatives, open all the Certificates, and the Votes shall then be counted. The. Person having the greatest Number of Votes shall be the President, if such Number be a majority of the whole Number of Electors appointed: and if there be more than one who have such Majority, and have an equal Number of Votes, then the House of Representatives shall immediately choose by Ballot one of them for President; and if no Person have a Majority, then from the five highest on the List the said House shall in like manner choose the President. But in choosing the President, the Votes shall be taken by States, the Representation from each State having one Vote; A quorum for this purpose shall consist of a Member or Members from two thirds of the States, and a Majority of all the States shall be necessary to a Choice. In every Case,after the Choice of the President, the Person having the greatest Number of Votes of the Electors shall be the Vice President. But if there should remain two or more who have equal Votes, the Senate shall chuse from them by Ballot the Vice President. (*This article was substantially changed by Amendment 12.)

Clause 4. The Congress may determine the Time of chusing the Electors, and the Day on which they shall give their Votes; which Day shall be the same throughout the United States.

The electoral college was one of the compromises by which the delegates were able to agree on the document finally produced. "This subject," said James Wilson, referring to the issue of the manner in which the president was to be selected, "has greatly divided the House, and will also divide people out of doors. It is in truth the most difficult of all on which we have had to decide."

Adoption of the electoral college plan came late in the convention, which had previously adopted on four occasions provisions for the election of the executive by the Congress and had twice defeated proposals for election by the people directly. Itself the product of compromise, the electoral college probably did not work as any member of the convention could have foreseen, because the development of political parties and the nomination of presidential candidates through them and designation of electors by the parties soon reduced the concept of the elector as an independent force to the vanishing point in practice if not in theory. But the electoral college concept remains despite numerous efforts to adopt another method. Indeed, it is a relic, but it is still a significant relic which must be dealt with every four years. Candidates running for president who give short shrift to the electoral college do not win.

State Elections

In a democracy, the election of leaders and representatives are the primary method for citizens to regularly influence and sometimes control the actions of their government. When voting does not provide the proper voice, citizens and residents frequently strike, riot, mobilize into mass marches, or organize coups d'états. Elections are crucial to a democracy—they legitimize officeholders and provide for reasonably smooth transitions of power and authority.

Essentially, beyond the presidential, there are five basic types of elections in American democracy: primary elections, general elections, initiatives/propositions, referenda, and recalls. Primaries are elections to select candidates for the general election (as are caucuses, or advertised general meetings of voters—the latter gathers to nominate and select candidates in a mass meeting). The major difference between a primary and a caucus is that the former is a scheduled election to choose candidates, while the latter is a mass meeting to select candidates.

Primaries and caucuses are usually held January through June. The general elections are usually scheduled for November. The general election is to choose between the available candidates (determined by primaries or caucuses) to fill the office-holding positions that are available.

There are closed primaries, which only allow persons registered in a particular party to vote to choose candidates to represent that party. Thus, in a closed primary, only registered Republicans can vote for Republicans, and only Democrats can vote in Democratic primaries. There are also open primaries, which allow independents, and sometimes cross-party voters. When the latter is allowed, it is called a crossover primary. In the latter, Democrats can vote to choose Republican candidates, and Republicans can choose Democratic candidates. There are also runoff primaries, which occur between the two largest voter-getters when no one got the simple majority of votes cast during the first primary.

The *initiative* is a device to give citizens more direct influence over legislation and public policy. A proposal of a specific piece of citizen-driven idea is put in a petition, a large number of signatures are gathered of registered voters supporting that proposal, the compiled list is turned into the Secretary of State's office, and if enough of the signatures are certified to meet the state's percentage requirement, the initiative gets on the ballot of either a primary or a general election. Once on the ballot, it is called a proposition.

A *referendum* is a state, county or city legislative decision that is then put on the public ballot for citizen re-approval. Legislative pay hikes, large bond measures, and the like are typical referendum items.

A *recall* is a de-election, or the unelecting of an official previously put in office. In America, everyone elected can be unelected except the president and vice president of the country. For those two, only the impeachment process is allowed. In order to force a recall, enough citizen-signed petitions must be submitted and certified.

Elections In California

A. Voting in California, as in other states, is a restricted franchise. Besides citizenship, it requires (a) age (of at least 18 years), (b) residency (at least fifteen days before an election one intends to vote in, although to vote for president and vice president of the U.S. fewer than fifteen days is allowable), (c) not to be either a convicted felon imprisoned at the time of the election on parole or probation, or (d) legally declared mentally incompetent.

B. English competency is not a requirement for voting in California, as determined by 1970s *Castro v. State of California*. Thus, voting ballots and other election-related materials in California are made available in Spanish, Chinese, Vietnamese, and English.

C. One must be properly registered in the election district in order to receive a ballot to vote on the day of the event. A registration form must be completed and submitted to the County Registrar of Voters fifteen days prior to the election in which one wants to participate.

D. To be a candidate for a publicly elected office, one must first be a registered voter. Those previously convicted of felonies, once their debt to society has been legally satisfied and they are no longer incarcerated, can petition to have their voting rights returned in California; most such requests, after proper investigation, are approved. Those in county jail not yet convicted of felonies are still eligible to register and to vote.

Voting Tips For November And Other Months: Decoding The California Voter Information Guide Without Losing One's Mind

Even though the sexy issue on the ballot for a particular year may not be like Barack Obama's first or second run for the White House were, there are really many more items that will affect Black folks and other people of color in California more immediately and sometimes more painfully. How do we decide intelligently which voting decision to make? The California Official Voter Information Guide that is sent out to all those registered to participate at the polls is currently over 140 pages of narrative, text, and intimidation. There are no pictures or cartoons to break the monopoly of semantics, so generally only the brave, retired, and have-no-other-life folk actually read this pamphlet (excluding political science students assigned the task). That's unfortunate, since the information contained is excellent and on point.

Here's some pragmatic, straight-ahead advice on how to utilize the voter guide beneficially. By the way, make sure to read and keep the Voter Bill of Rights printed on page 143 of the pamphlet. For the propositions, which are usually the bulk of the ballot in California, go straight to the Legislative Analyst's Report in the voter guide at the beginning of each proposition. Look especially at "The Proposal" and "The Effects." You can ignore everything else if you want, but then go backwards in the pamphlet to the Quick Reference Guide section, which is a summary of everything about each proposition.

A. Follow the GENERAL PRINCIPLES (always ask the following questions about voting propositions):

1. Will this proposition help my primary group? (Ethnic Group, Gender Group, etc.) (If yes, consider voting yes; if no, vote no.)
2. Will it harm my primary group? (If yes, clearly vote no; if no, ask more questions.)
3. Will it help me as an individual? (If yes, vote yes; if no, consider more questions.)
4. Will it harm me as an individual? (If yes, immediately vote no; if no, consider the other questions.)
5. Who is accountable for making sure the proposition is done the way it says? (If that is not explained, vote no.)

B. If looking at a bond measure, always see who is responsible for making sure the money is spent on what it promises to be spent on—if no one is responsible, or that issue is vague, vote no. If you have to pay more for the bond measure, and it's not about school, fire/police, etc., vote no.

C. If all else fails, you can always wait for Congressperson Maxine Waters' list (or someone like her) of what to vote for, although you should decide on your own. Be an informed voter.

Chapter Thirteen

Interest Groups and Political Influence

Interest groups in American politics provide regular opportunities for citizens and other residents to influence public decision-making to one degree or another. They most frequently work in the spaces not filled by registered political party activities and, especially through the Internet, take their advocacies straight to the government policy makers. Interest groups provide the opportunity for non-represented and under-represented bodies of people—ethnic, racial, aged, social, neighborhood, non-profit, etc.—to get their voices heard and their issues addressed. Clearly, tactics and strategies used by interest groups aimed at influencing public policy vary, from letter writing, phoning officials, canvassing, campaigning for candidates, protest marches, media interviews and blogs, celebrity concerts, political rallies, lobbying, bum rushing meetings that political leaders attend, town halls, caucuses, law suits, etc., there are several common denominators identifiable for successful interest group efforts in America and in California.

First, interest groups can be defined as large or small collections of individuals who join forces based on sharing one or several political goals or needs that they think they can accomplish by influencing decision-making related to those goals within the political arena. All successful interest groups must be able to consistently define, articulate, advocate, and defend their interests, and they must be able to organize their members strategically to carry out relevant tasks. Unorganized groups are rarely successful in American politics—they can make noise, but sound and fury alone don't get the job done. The level of organized energy and effort focused relentlessly on a particular goal is functionally related to a group's success in accomplishing its political mission and having its needs addressed. Simply having political self-righteousness or even political correctness on one's side does not ensure or even predict success. Successful interest groups must be able to target their efforts, maximize their resources, dedicate themselves to resiliency and flexibility in the face of opposition, and, once confident on the path or approach they've decided upon, never give up. Politics is not about fairness; it is about articulation, focus, and finishing.

There are multiple issue groups and single issue groups. There are relatively permanent organizations of these groups, and temporary mobilizations of these groups for specific time related purposes. Essentially, there are three main types of interest groups regularly operating in American politics: economic interest groups (i.e., groups seeking to influence policy related to their members' financial benefit, be it tax reduction, increased commercial opportunities, easing regulations that interfere in profit-making; or increasing subsidies, such as chambers of commerce, labor unions, and farmers' associations); public interest groups (those who focus their activities on achieving collective benefits for society at large rather than rewards for their own membership, such as Common Cause, Prisoners' Rights, Children's Defense Fund, Societies for the Prevention of HIV/AIDS, etc.), and lobbying groups (i.e., those who are paid to influence lawmakers and decision-makers). Though the latter, lobbying, is a term often used for volunteer efforts, large or small, essentially lobbying is a legally defined term in California (California Political Reform Act, 1974) and other states that refers to paid professional or non professional influence activities.

Currently, there are over 2,000 registered lobbyists working in California as individual consultants for particular groups or as groups themselves representing the interests of over 3,500 California associations and organizations, ranging from education interests to agriculture, energy production and distribution , transportation, the legal community, finance/insurance, railroads, health-related groups, labor organizations, etc.

Non-governmental organizations (NGO), which are also called civil society organizations, and community-based organizations (CBOs) dominate the non-profit sectors of public interest groups in California and elsewhere.

Chapter Fourteen

Politics in California

I n California, as in other states, the 10th Amendment to the U.S. Constitution provides:

A.   The authority to establish and control state, county, city and district government

B.   The authority to regularly schedule and conduct elections

C.   The authority to establish and legitimize business corporations

D.   The authority to establish state civil and criminal laws

E.   The authority to organize and utilize police powers

California has the largest U.S. congressional representation in the country, with fifty-five members of Congress (and thus, fifty-five electoral college votes). This large number is based on California having the largest current population in the country, and it is growing. After 2012, California's congressional delegation may equal fifty-six or fifty-seven based on increased population.

At the federal representation level, California is divided into two U.S. Senate districts and fifty-three U.S. House districts, with the lower numbers being in Northern and Central California and the higher numbers being in Southern California. For example, U.S. House District 7 is in Northern California, and House District 35 is in Southern California.

At the state level, there is a State Senate, with forty members, and a State Assembly with eighty members. Thus, there are forty State Senate districts in California, and eighty Assembly districts. The same geographical influences apply as mentioned above.

At the county level, each of the fifty-eight counties in California has its own government, budget, authority, and public policy. Generally, there are from three to seven elected county supervisors who hire a county administrator to oversee the day-to-day administration of the government.

At the city level, California has 478 incorporated cities, each with either a general law pattern of government or a charter-city style. General law mandates an elected city council and a hired city manager. Charter cities can choose their style of government. In California, the choices are from STRONG MAYOR, MODERATE MAYOR, and WEAK MAYOR forms. The first provides the mayor the authority to override the decisions of city/county administrators, veto budgets, fire department heads, etc. Only San Francisco, currently, has that type. The second, typified by Los Angeles, provides the mayor authority over a large number of city commissions and limited veto powers over city council legislation. Essentially, however, there is a separation of powers between the mayor, as the executive, and the city council, as the legislative body. The city council of elected representatives controls the municipal budget and other major items. In the last type, the mayor is simply the presiding officer of the city council. Essentially, the city is run by the hired city manager (hired by the city council).

California has eleven constitutional officers—that is, eleven state-wide officers elected at-large over the state (some say twelve based on the complexities of one office). These are:

A.   Governor
B.   Lt. Governor
C.   Secretary of State
D.   Treasurer
E.   Controller
F.   Insurance Commissioner
G.   State Attorney General
H.   State Schools Superintendent
I.   State Board of Equalization (four members, one of whom is the State Controller)

Referendum, Initiative and Recall

Referendum, Initiative, and Recall are used as direct democracy more frequently in California than in any other state. There is a prevailing distrust of elected governmental leadership in this state.

A. Recalls are elections to unelect a government official, and all duly elected representatives in the state are subject to that process, from district water board personnel to judges to governors. In order to recall an official, there is first a qualifying stage. That phase requires citizens who are advocating the removal of an elected person either to properly notify the county clerk in which the official serves or the California secretary of state's office that an effort to recall that particular elected representative will be made. A brief statement explaining the rationale for the recall must also be submitted. Subsequently, a recall petition must be circulated among registered voters within a legally specified time period. If the proper number of signatures is obtained within the allowable time period, part two of the process—the election stage—begins.

B. At a designated election paid for by the government, voters are asked, "Shall Mr./Ms. X be removed from the office to which he/she has been duly elected?" A simple majority of "Yes" votes is required for the person to be voted out of office. Usually on the same ballot, there are names of candidates to replace the official if the recall is successful. The person being recalled cannot have his/her name on that list of candidates. However, if a simple majority is not obtained to remove the representative, then all names of replacement candidates are deleted and become null and void. If the recall is successful, the winning candidate only needs a plurality to achieve victory, not a majority.

C. To recall a statewide officer in California, petitioners need signatures from no less than 12% of the last public vote count for that representative's office; if it is an executive office (governor, insurance commissioner, etc.), the signatures must be obtained within 160 days from filing the notice to recall. If a legislative officer (assembly, state senate), the signatures of 20% of the vote count in the last election for that position and 160 days to collect them; and if a judicial representative, the same requirements as the legislative officer. For local representatives, the numbers are 30% and 40 days (in cities, towns or districts less than 1,000 population); 25% and up to 90 days (cities, towns or districts of 10,000 or fewer); 20% and 120 days (population between 10,000 and 50,000); and up to 15% and 160 days (with population over 50,000).

D. Referenda (singular, "referendum") are ballot measures at either the state level or the local/county level. At the state level, the measures are identified by a number (e.g., Prop 13), and at the local/county level, with a letter (e.g., Measure C). In California, there are three basic types of referenda: compulsory referenda, advisory referenda, and protest referenda. The first two are put on the ballot by elected officials, and the latter by citizen petitioners.

E. Any legislative act passed in the state that places California in debt (e.g. highway construction bonds), proposed constitutional amendments or changes to city or county charters, and proposed legislative amendments to ballot measures already passed by California citizens (e.g., changes to the Three Strikes law) must be placed immediately and automatically on the ballot for voter approval or rejection. These are called compulsory referenda and are government-initiated. An advisory referendum is a measure placed on the ballot by government officials to find out how people feel about a proposed idea. It is also called a straw poll, and has no legal or binding effect. Neither of these two referenda needs, nor will use, petition drives. The third type, the protest referenda, is a citizen-driven opposition to some law approved by the legislature and signed by the governor (at the state level), or passed by county, city, or district government. The protest referendum seeks to nullify and make moot a particular law and it requires a petition with the signatures of registered voters equal to at least 5% of those who voted in the last governor's race (gubernatorial contest) in California in order to be placed on the ballot for voter approval or rejection, for statewide issues, or for mayor in municipal issues. Petitioners only have the first ninety days after the law has been implemented in order to collect the required signatures or the protest is canceled.

F. Citizen Initiatives/Propositions are the clearest examples of direct democracy, in that once on the ballot and approved by voters, the propositions by-pass both the governor's signature and passage by the state legislature. In other words, state executive or legislative approval is not necessary. The only statewide branch of government that can dilute or nullify citizen initiatives/propositions approved by the voters is the judiciary. However, in order to have the courts look at a citizen ballot measure, a case must be filed and brought into the judicial system as a violation of either the state or the federal constitution. The courts will not automatically evaluate or judicially review any citizen-sponsored ballot measure in California. There are two basic kinds of initiatives (called this while at the petition stage) or propositions (what initiatives are called once they are on the ballot): *initiative constitutional amendments* (aka, constitutional initiatives), and *initiative statutes* (aka, statute initiatives).

G. The constitutional amendment initiative/proposition is aimed at adding a law to the California State Constitution. Once drafted by a small committee (if not just one person), the petitioner(s) give notice of intent to collect signatures (to the secretary of state) and begin gathering signatures, either by a body of volunteers, or by paid signature-gatherers. The petitioners must collect enough signatures of registered voters to equal no less than 8% of the voters in the last California governor's race to get the initiative on the ballot, and they must do so within 150 days of filing the intent. The statute initiative, aimed at changing the California statutory code, must get at least 5% of the registered voters in the last gubernatorial election within 150 days after filing the intent in order to be placed on the ballot.

Chapter Fifteen

Politics in California

Neighborhood Empowerment Councils: L.A.'s "Secret" Power Base

A dmittedly, one can become entirely too blasé about expecting any beginning "Intro to Politics" students to dazzle their teacher with their basic knowledge of who their California federal, state legislative, county supervisorial, city council, and district school board representatives are (the same goes for virtually every other state, too).

They even have trouble with the eight Los Angeles Community College board members, and those names are in every class schedule, and their big portraits hang right outside the library, seemingly staring straight at every student coming in or out of the building.

Unlike the eleven or so statewide officers who represent all of California, these others are the directly elected voices (for neighborhoods, districts, and streets) in the public policy engagements, so when the current crop of young charges are not up on this knowledge from Jump Street, teachers may have to regularly carve out time in class to pour this foundation cement for their political house.

One has to accept that now as a S.O.P.(standard operating procedure) chore. However, what is even more amazing is the general lack of recognition and irritation that occurs once the topic becomes Los Angeles' Neighborhood Councils/Neighborhood Empowerment Zones (NC). The teacher may as well be speaking Swahili or Wolof.

This is not simply a case of student apathy and nonchalance. The general public in Los Angeles, most especially the overwhelming majority of the Black population in the city, is clueless. If you mention Frank Prater, or Jacquelyn Dupont-Walker, Saundra Bryant or even Brother Julian Rogers, unless you are talking to long-term municipal activists, you can bet the farm that nobody but you will have the slightest idea who and what you are talking about. Are they athletes? Are they part of 100 Black Men, the African Marketplace, or Congressperson Waters' staff? No, none of the above, although each is highly accomplished and still going strong.

They, and a handful of other like-minded Black folk, are participants in what some call the Neighborhood Council Movement in Los Angeles. Notice what was said though: a handful of Black folk, while literally thousands of Whites, Asians, and Latinos are involved in making decisions that affect the public on a regular basis.

OK, you say, so what? How's that different from a whole lot of what goes on in L.A.? We are always overrepresented in the going-to-jail or prison population, in the dropping-out-of-school population, and in the poor, broke, and where-is-my-check population. So, that just sounds like one more population we can avoid and shouldn't worry about.

The problem is, as stated before, Black folk are simply not taking care of their political busness well in this modern environment. The Black community consistently elects Black folk to represent it, but most frequently end up with people who look Black but who merely acquiesce to greed, unethical behavior, and/or poor representation of that community.

As a population in Los Angeles, Blacks are constantly being outmaneuvered, left out, left behind, and ignored. Remember the fight over the railway next to Dorsey High? They (the powers that be) can see members of the Black community coming to march a little, vent a lot, have a prayer vigil, and then they watch and expect Black folk to merely drop it and go home, which they regularly do. Putting consistent leveraged influence on our city and county policy makers is simply not what the Black community does. It has mastered reacting, responding, and then moving on until the next crisis. That's a formula for political oblivion, and right now that's the high cotton the Southern California Black community lives in.

The neighborhood council authorization goes back to the voter-approved revision of the L.A. City Charter in 1999, Article IX, Section 901(c).

Ostensibly, that provision was a belated response to the Valley succession movement and the argument that city government, then, was too insular and exclusive. After a slow start, neighborhood councils (NCs) now have become a solid, basic unit of L.A. government administration.

True, the powers of the NC are essentially advisory, but collective NC action has already stopped the Department of Water and Power pay raises and several other major decisions the public did not like.

Currently, there is a very strong set of advocacies for the full formation and operation of a Congress of Neighborhood Councils in L.A. to collaboratively bring community influence and clout regularly to city-government decisions. The L.A. Neighborhood Council Coalition (LANCC), presently with forty-two of the ninety-one certified Neighborhood Councils as members, is rapidly becoming synonymous with the Congress of Councils, although there are others cropping up like the South L.A. Alliance of Neighborhood Councils to show that complete unity is not yet a fact. Either way, the Black voices are almost negligible.

Still, why should Black folk care? Many did not vote one way or the other for the new city charter. For one thing, the Black community (and other communities of color) should care and get involved as quickly as possible, because it is through those neighborhood councils that much street maintenance, rock-house removal, tree trimming, community renovation, and the like are being recommended and handled. In fact, a typical response from the district offices of the 8th, 9th, or 10th council districts regarding such issues is, "Have you run it through your NC?" So, what we are talking about here is a neighborhood group annually provided with upwards of $45,000 in city funds to both advise downtown and take actions on its own.

The second reason involvement is so important is that it provides free on-the-job training in political leadership. For those who even think they want to run for public office, here is a "magical" neighborhood incubator for getting prepared to do so. The city department charged with the responsibility of monitoring, maintaining, and assessing neighborhood councils, the Department of Neighborhood Empowerment (DONE), even regularly offers free classes in its Empowerment L.A. Leadership Institute. That's a gimme that the Black community should take advantage of.

However, there's that other part of the problem implied—even if inspired by something or someone to get up and get involved, how and where do you do that? Yes, they do act like it's some sort of secret. Those who know know; those who don't, probably won't. The DONE mentioned above is supposed to do community outreach and educate the public on NCs.

However, the department's website is wack. Although citizens are known to put in the computer time to find and play video games, to investigate gossip and Hollywood rumors, or just to get to pornography, they will consistently click only two or three times to find out information pertaining to government.

If the data does not flow almost instantaneously, too bad, they're gone. The DONE's website lists wonderful icons and links, like cable franchise maps, public safety contacts and tips, loans for home buyers, and other important announcements. However, when people try to click on "How Do I Get Involved" and "Where Exactly Is My Neighborhood Council," they most frequently get a set of fumbling links that just frustrate them. Wow.

They're motivated, but can't find out where to go. Ah, well, and then they're off to something else, a valuable opportunity lost because of faulty or deliberately misleading data distribution. Another political asset hidden in plain sight.

And, the information and NC operations did not just arrive. They have been around for more than ten years, and the NCs of 2010 are really in the mix of city government, but mainly without large-scale Black involvement and participation.

Right now, the single best source of quick, reliable information about the Neighborhood Council Movement and why more of the public should be involved is the website for the Neighborhood Council Review Commission, at *www.ncrcla.org*. That commission has been evaluating the impact of NCs in Los Angeles, and its first report is already out and available to the public. The Black community is urged to investigate that source. Wake up and get up, folks. Political windows of opportunity are closing on those ill-prepared and ill-informed, and some communities do not even seem to notice.

Political oblivion awaits.

Chapter Sixteen

President Obama and the Black Political Agenda

O n Tuesday, January 25, 2011, President Barack Obama delivered his second State of the Union address, as called for by the U.S. Constitution. This was also his fourth speech to a joint session of Congress.

It was hoped that there would be no more of the egregiously disrespectful conduct exhibited by South Carolina Congressman Joe Wilson, with his "You lie" outburst (an unprecedented violation for which he received a mere hand-slap penalty from the House of Representatives) the previous year.

However, there had admittedly been a strong reaction from the right to Obama's massive legislative successes of the past two years. This gave rise to the Tea Party phenomenon, and Obama himself acknowledged that he and the Democratic Party took "a shellacking" during the November 2010 elections in which the GOP took over the House.

Many Democrats feared that President Obama and the party's hands would be tied for the next two years, and they were correct in that concern. But Democrats have much to applaud already in one of the most productive legislative periods on record.

Will the shellacking be followed by a shackling of Obama's legislative agenda? This leader has impressed with his skill, and it's unlikely that we won't see flashes of those skills in the coming months.

As the first African-American to attain the highest office in the land, President Obama can legitimately claim many accomplishments along the pathway of change in and for America during the 24 months since his inauguration. Troops are steadily being drawn down from the Iraq military adventure without panic or loss of face, as occurred in Vietnam.

The Lillie Ledbetter legislation the president signed has provided the strongest legal basis yet for comparable worth in the workplace for American women.

There are new regulations on credit card companies. There is a relatively strong set of regulations and constraints regarding financial institutions and consumer protection in the U.S. Financial Reform Act. All these measures, the White House staff says, help all of America, including the Black community.

During the 2011 speech, which will probably be great oratory, what can Black Americans expect to hear? And, more importantly, what can they expect in tangible terms from the next two years of Barack Obama's first term?

The most practical answer to both questions regarding our most pragmatic of presidents is very probably more of the same.

That "same" means a thick mesh of third- or fourth-page news-producing decisions that have benefited the Black community in distinctive ways, with one or two headline-crashing exceptions to that rule. That "same" means the president will not specifically target in public the goals, projects, and activities he wants done to satisfy demands of the Black community. The tasks and projects just get done without fanfare or bombast.

For example, with the 2010 Executive Order and the corresponding White House initiative on HBCUs, nearly $100 million became available to HBCUs in the 2011 budget, along with financial access to regular annual federal support for an expanded list of these schools, all not available to them since the Lyndon Johnson era. Few but insiders knew. A second example is the Claims Resolution Act of 2010, which appropriated monies to settle the Cobell Indian lawsuit and the Pigford II Black farmers' lawsuit, although this one was publicized a little more widely than other such efforts by President Obama.

As a matter of fact, if one did a random selection quiz of most Americans, as one recent poll did, very few even among the president's supporters can name ten of the most significant executive orders, pieces of legislation, senior appointments, or other tangible results scored by the Obama presidency. In the Black community, which still supports the president heavily in spite of rhetoric to the contrary, that percentage is even lower.

How then can Blacks expect more, when there is no regular assessment of what has already been done? The answer may lie in the nature of that expectation.

Two Angelenos from different generations interviewed recently on this issue—Robbye Davis and Opal Young—put it this way: "Our president has not embarrassed us. He has been prudent, ethical, a gentleman and a brilliant political scholar. He may very well be too smart for them. Black folks need their leaders, particularly in this case THE leader, not to make them put their heads down in shame. The president has good home training, and he makes us proud. We expect him to keep on that path. Just stay on the high road."

Additionally, the very symbol of President Obama and the First Family being in the White House still holds sway among virtually all Blacks, both inside and outside of the U.S.A.

Internet mail continues to demonstrate President Obama's tremendous international reputation and popularity. He is still the reference point for breaking the greatest glass ceiling of the Black community's life experiences. To many in the Black community, it is enough that according to the stats, President Obama has accomplished more on the progressive agenda in two years than both Misters Bush did in twelve.

So, even without being able to recite a substantial portion of the president's accomplishments, it just feels like he's doing all right, several community denizens added. "He's a credit to the race, and we expect he will continue to be. For me, that's enough. Long as they don't Arizona him, he'll be fine," said a Mr. Roberts.

But whether some in the Black community still demand that the president lay out and subscribe to a specific Black agenda or not, given the perpetual state of the Black American population—17 percent unemployment, high prison incarceration and recidivism rates, high HIV-related deaths, high mortgage foreclosures, high drop-out rates, lowered average life expectancy, high urban criminal statistics, and other negatives—there will continue to be scrutiny and assessment of President Obama as long as he is anywhere close to the reins of American political leadership.

For example, every president gets the Census Bureau End of Term Assessment, eventually. That means this president, too, will be measured based on whether the average American made progress or lost ground during his administration.

The 2009 version of that report evaluated George W. Bush's administration and found that he left America substantially worse off than he found it when he came in as president in 2000. The standard indices of that evaluation, including median household income, level of poverty, childhood poverty, and the number of citizens without health insurance, demonstrated that Bush essentially flunked the presidential course, earning the dubious distinction, according to the Economic Policy Institute, of being the only known American head of state to have led the country into eight years of economic decline. The median income declined, overall poverty increased, as did childhood poverty to alarming proportions, and there was a major increase in the number of Americans without health insurance and the means to fend off catastrophic illness.

When George H.W. Bush left office in 1992, the median American income was $46,603; when Bill Clinton left office in 2000; it was $52,500, and when George W. Bush left, it was down 4.2 percent to $50,303.

The number of Americans living in poverty when G. H. W. Bush left office was 38 million; when Clinton left it was down 6.4 percent to 31.6 million; but when G. W. Bush left in 2008, that number had increased by 21.6 percent.

Children in poverty declined under Clinton and increased under Bush, the younger, and those without health insurance declined under Clinton and increased under Bush.

It is entirely too early to do this kind of in-depth assessment of Obama's presidency. But using the current indices, he just might do all right. Those indices are clearly towards the positive right now.

But for those wanting to evaluate President Obama today, or those who want to refute negative claims of President Obama's achievements thus far in office, here's a list of accomplishments that specifically benefit the Black community:

Legislation Advocated, Supported, and Signed

1. Got unemployment benefits extended for another thirteen months so more than 3.5 million Americans could continue getting monies for food, housing, and other essentials. Black Americans are a significant part of that population.
2. Got payroll taxes and taxes on small businesses reduced so more money is in people's pockets, and there is more incentive for small businesses to hire folk.
3. Got the Black Farmers' $1.3 billion reparations lawsuit against the federal government settled for the farmers.
4. Signed legislation to protect college students from predatory lenders and onerous pay-back schemes, and signing major legislation reducing the debt-burden of college student loans.
5. Signed the Fair Sentencing Act of 2010, which drastically decreases the impact of disproportionate mandatory/minimum sentencing for first-time drug abusers and those convicted of simple possession. A large number of Black American men and women are currently incarcerated because of these old-school "Rockefeller Laws," and many more were on the way. This legislation is a substantial step in the right direction to quell that major population increase in Black incarceration.
6. Signed the repeal of "Don't Ask, Don't Tell," after having already signed an executive order declaring assaults against gays as hate crimes. There are Black members of the gay and lesbian community in the military who are positively affected by this.
7. Signed the first significant piece of legislation in nearly 100 years that called for comparable-worth pay in the workplace (the Lillie Ledbetter Act). This includes Black women in the workplace.
8. Authorized a $789 billion economic stimulus plan, which included one third of its authorization as tax cuts for working-class and middle-income families, one third to states for infrastructure construction projects, and one third to states to prevent the layoff of police officers, teachers, and other civil servants at risk of losing their jobs because of city and state budget shortfalls.
9. Authorized and signing legislation that changes the relationship between credit card companies and the card-holding public. This

includes banning the raising of rates arbitrarily and without advance notification, especially if customers are paying bills on time.

10. Signed legislation to fully fund the U.S. Department of Veterans Affairs for the first time since 1956 to honor our commitment to returning and former soldiers. America has a large number of Black veterans.

11. Signed the historic Wall Street reform bill that was designed to put in new regulations and federal oversight to end the kind of abusive practices that helped start and fuel the current recession, and to promote consumer safety through the presence of a powerful Consumer Protection Commission.

12. Promised to sign legislation establishing the Promise Neighborhood Program introduced by a member of the CBC.

13. Re-funded arts education nationally in public schools. Black children and teaching adults are included as beneficiaries.

14. Fully funded the National Endowment for the Arts for the first time since President Jimmy Carter's administration. Black creative folk— writers, painters, sculptors—benefit from this too.

15. Signed the Matthew Shepard and James Byrd, Jr. Hate Crimes Prevention Act that made it a federal crime to assault an individual because of his or her sexual orientation or gender identity.

16. Signed the Helping Families Save Their Homes Act, which expanded the *Making Home Affordable Program* to help millions of Americans avoid preventable foreclosures. It also provided $2.2 billion to help combat homelessness and to help stabilize the overall housing market.

17. Tripled the federal budget resources to hire more FDA meat inspectors, another job opportunity for Black workers.

18. Signed the re-authorization and updating of the Violence Against Women Act, first passed in 1994. The VAWA has provided funding to states and local communities to develop specialized law enforcement units, provide services to victims, and improve prosecution for sexual assault, physical abuse and other such crimes. Since the passage of the act, the annual incidence of domestic violence has dropped by more than 50 percent. This law includes federal protection for Black women.

19. Authorized, through the Credit Card Accountability, Responsibility, and Disclosure (CARD) Act, new consumer protections that terminated the previous practice of protecting only credit card companies at the expense of consumers.

20. Signed legislation that re-authorized and expanded the SCHIP program, the State Children's Health Insurance Program, in February 2009, to cover healthcare for 11 million children, over 4 million of them uninsured. This was prior to the new Affordable Healthcare Act, and recognized as the first positive step in that direction. A large number of the uninsured children targeted by the legislation are Black.

21. Authorized tangible tax credits to first-time home buyers through the Worker, Homeownership, and Business Assistance Act of 2009 to help revitalize the U.S. housing market.

22. Authorized the largest spending increase in 30 years to the Department of Veterans Affairs to improve medical facilities and national cemeteries, and to assist states in acquiring or constructing state nursing homes and extended-care facilities for those who fought for America. This was part of the Veterans Health Care Budget Reform and Transparency Act, which establishes advance appropriations for the Department of Veterans Affairs by providing two-fiscal year budget authority rather than year-by-year, thus enabling better medical care planning for veterans. This process was endorsed by the American Legion, American Veterans, Blinded Veterans Association, Disabled American Veterans, Jewish War Veterans, Military Officers Association, Military Order of the Purple Heart, Paralyzed Veterans of America, and Vietnam Veterans of America, which is one of the first times that kind of agreement has been achieved. Also through this act, the president appointed the first Special Assistant to the President for Disability Policy.

23. Authorized actions to protect 300,000 education jobs, such as teachers, principals, librarians, and counselors through the American Recovery Act that would have otherwise been lost.

24. Authorized the extension of discounted COBRA health coverage for the nation's unemployed from nine months to fifteen months, so that workers laid off between September 1, 2008 and February 28, 2010 would qualify for affordable temporary healthcare.

25. Authorized through the SBA and the American Recovery and Investment Act $14.7 billion in new small business loans as of Nov. 13, 2009. Twenty percent of that went to minority-owned firms, 26 percent to rural firms, 19 percent to women-owned firms, and 9 percent to veteran-owned firms.

26. Authorized, through the important Edward M. Kennedy Serve America Act, a major expansion of the volunteer National Service and the National Youth Service Programs. Properly utilized, both of these projects provide excellent alternative skills training for public sector employment for Black folk who avail themselves of the opportunity.

Presidential Executive Orders:

1. Signed an executive order to implement the President's Initiative on Historically Black Colleges and Universities, and directly increasing the federal financial support of HBCUs, together allowing a significant number of those colleges to stave off bankruptcy.

2. Ordered FEMA and the EPA to once again report directly to the president, ending the mismanagement cycle for natural disasters and environmental issues seen during the Bush Administration (remember Katrina?).

3. Ordered the White House and all federal agencies to respect the Freedom of Information Act, thereby overturning Bush-era limits on accessibility of federal documents. This helps Black researchers, intellectuals, and activists.

4. Made significant cracks in the old boys' network of constant contract procurement by ending no-bid federal contracting; banning tax delinquent and tax non-payment individuals and companies from bidding on federal contracts; ordering the removal and banning of lobbyists from serving on federal and White House advisory panels and boards; and ordering the Open Government Directive, which mandates all cabinet departments to advocate, promote, and implement public transparency and citizen participation in department initiatives.

5. Authorized the U.S. auto industry rescue plan and two GMAC rescue packages that essentially saved GM and Chrysler, and thus thousands of auto industry jobs, including those belonging to many Black Americans.

6. Changed NASA's current and future mission and tripled its funding. There are significant numbers of Blacks working for NASA in a variety of positions.

7. Doubled the monies available for Pell Grants. This is a significant benefit for all college-bound students, including Black students.

8. Resurrected funding and respect for the EEOC, which investigates racial discrimination in the workplace.

9. Authorized a major increase in AmeriCorps, a national Peace Corps-like volunteer service created during the Clinton Administration in 1993. Through it, Americans can learn usable skills while they help other Americans conquer illiteracy, improve healthcare, build affordable houses, learn computer competency, clean parks and streams, etc. Those accepted in the program full-time earn money for college and can get waiver credits for student loans.

10. Authorized the beginning of a new national policy on Cuba, allowing Cuban families to return home to visit loved ones, and recently, allowing close to full release of the ban on travel to Cuba. There are significant numbers of Black Cubans in America.

11. Authorized removing restrictions on embryonic stem-cell research so cures for significant diseases can be found.

12. Authorized having all transportation expenses of the families of fallen soldiers covered so those families can be on hand when the body arrives at Dover AFB.

13. Authorized ending the media blackout on war casualties so that reporters can provide transparent, full information, including covering the return of fallen soldiers to Dover AFB within respectful rules and the approval of a fallen soldier's family.

14. Allocated special funding to the Labor Department to provide green job training to veterans, which includes Black folk.

15. Directed the DEA to relax drug enforcement of national marijuana laws in order to encourage states that legalized medical marijuana to regulate themselves. Fourteen states have allowed some use of marijuana for medical purposes: Alaska, California, Colorado, Hawaii, Maryland, Michigan, Montana, Nevada, New Mexico, Oregon, Maryland, Rhode Island, Vermont, and Washington. In California and other states, growing medical marijuana is a new income stream for Black farmers, among others.

16. Authorized a federal crackdown on companies that denied sick pay, vacation time, and health insurance to workers by abusing the employee classification system through claiming those employees as

independent contractors. Such companies were also avoiding paying Social Security, Medicare, and unemployment insurance taxes for those workers. A significant number of Black workers were in this employment situation.

17. Issued an executive order to create the National Commission on Fiscal Responsibility and Reform, including a Director of Consumer Protection. This led to the Financial Reform Act.

18. Signed an Executive Order establishing a White House Council on Women and Girls in order to provide a coordinated federal response to the challenges confronted by women and girls in trying to forge successful careers, and to direct that all cabinet and cabinet-level agencies consider how their policies and programs impact women and families.

19. Authorized the necessary funding for the design of a new Smithsonian National Museum of African American History, which is scheduled to open on the National Mall in 2015.

20. Authorized lowering drug costs for seniors and ended the previous practice of forbidding Medicare from negotiating with drug manu-facturers for cheaper drugs; the federal government is now realizing hundreds of millions in savings in that area. Having access to cheaper generic and prescription drugs is a benefit to the Black community, with our many health issues.

21. Authorized increasing the pay and benefits for military personnel, and for improving and upgrading the housing for military personnel. Many Black folk are in the American military.

22. Authorized the initiation of a new policy to promote greater federal hiring of military spouses in order to utilize a mass of under-used talent.

23. Authorized the ending of the previous policy of giving tax benefits to corporations that outsourced American jobs; the new policy promotes in-sourcing to bring jobs back.

24. Authorized (taking a substantial risk in doing so) the rescue plan for GM and Chrysler Automakers. Its success saved the auto industry and thousands of American jobs, many of them held by Black Americans.

Presidential Appointments

1. Appointed (and getting ratified) two remarkable women to the United States Supreme Court, Justice Sonia Sotomayor, the first Hispanic woman on the Court, and Justice Elena Kagan. No, they are not Black, but they are more sensitive to issues of people of color than are most others on the Court.

2. Authorized the immediate reinstatement of 100 thousand federal employees (many of whom are Black).

3. Appointed the most gender- and ethnic-diversity-based presidential cabinet in history, including more women appointees than any other incoming president. Blacks represent ten of forty-five current senior cabinet and White House presidential assistant or commission positions, including Attorney General Eric Holder; EPA Executive Administrator Lisa P. Jackson; UN Ambassador Susan Rice; Senior Presidential Adviser Valerie Jarrett; Surgeon General Dr. Regina Benjamin; EEOC Director Jacquelyn Berrien, Director, EEOC; Council of Economic Advisers Member Dr. Cecilia E. Rouse; Deputy Assistant to the President and Director of Policy for the First Lady Jocelyn Frye; Director of the Domestic Policy Council Melody Barnes; Deputy Director of Legislative Affairs for VP Biden Nicole Isaac; Commissioner of the Food and Drug Administration Margaret Hamburg; and Advisory Council on Financial Capability A. Barry Rand.

4. Appointed the highest percentage of women, Blacks (21 percent of appointments), and other ethnic groups to federal judgeships compared to any previous president.

5. Appointed one of the largest percentages of federal employees who are Black compared to any previous president during his first term.

*During Black History Month 2011 and 2012, President Obama and First Lady Michelle Obama have hosted more Black performers and creative innovators in the White House than any previous president. During 2012, for example, every weekend of February saw a different coterie of Black and other performers providing praise and celebration to Black History, including a dynamic Motown Revue and performances by blues masters Buddy Guy and B.B. King, as well as by Mick Jagger and others.

This cultural component is exceedingly important in spreading the word from a national pulpit that Black American culture is alive, pulsating, and still very, very much in the spirit of expanding the Black Experience. Additionally, President Obama gets credit for helping to bring to fruition both the MLK Memorial and the Smithsonian Institute's African American Museum of History and Culture, the latter being the first national effort of this magnitude, to be built in a brand new, futuristic facility right on the Washington Mall.

Glossary

Some Basic Political Science Definitions

1. Political Science and Politics: See pp. 1–5.
2. Politics and the Scientific Method: See pp. 1-2.
3. The Mayflower Compact: The first written example of representative democracy in the American English colonies, 1620. It established a restricted franchise as a part of American democracy—that is, one has to be eligible and qualified to vote. In this case, one had to be a male member of the Church of England (Anglicans) over the age of twelve.
4. House of Burgesses: The first established example of a locally elected assembly in the English colonies, 1619. This was in Jamestown, Virginia. Burgesses are merchants. The local constituency elected people from their own neighborhoods.
5. Common Law: Judge-made law, that is, rules and principles decided upon in the field in traditional English life, and not usually based on precedents or prior cases. From that tradition, American law took such principles of common law as the *writ of habeas corpus*.
6. Ratification: There are two main types of ratification in American government—re-approval by the U.S. Senate of all presidential appointments to the U.S. federal court (including the Supreme Court), all treaties, and all appointments to the president's cabinet; and state legislature re-approval of an amendment to the U.S. Constitution after Congress and the President of the U.S. have already approved

it. The Articles of Confederation had to be approved by unanimity (unanimous vote or 100 percent) of the states, all thirteen at the time. The second U.S. Constitution and all subsequent constitutional amendments have had to be re-approved by 75 percent (three fourths) of the states.

7. Articles of Confederation: America's first written Constitution, passed in 1776 and not ratified until 1781–1783. It was written and approved by the Second Continental Congress, America's first national government.

8. Myths of American Government: A myth is a belief based on very few, if any, facts and a lot of embellishment or exaggeration. Standard myths of American government include equality is guaranteed for every citizen, freedom of speech allows people to say anything at anytime, all citizens can vote, America is a classless society (classes do not exist), racism is dead in America, and that impeachment of a president always means removing him from office.

9. Continental Congresses I and II: CCI was an elected body, meeting in Philadelphia and representing all thirteen colonies. In 1774, the CCI sent English King George a letter fervently requesting that he and the British soldiers (the colonial police) treat the colonists like the full-fledged English citizens that they were. King George refused them better treatment. In 1775–1776, the CCII met and dissolved their colonial ties to England by declaring all thirteen colonies as independent states bound together as the United States of America. The CCII wrote the Articles of Confederation and assigned Thomas Jefferson and Ben Franklin to write the first draft of the Declaration of Independence.

10. Differences Between the Articles of Confederation and the U.S. Constitution: The AOC had a weak central government that could not raise revenue, could not declare war, could not raise its own army, could not regulate trade between states, and could not print its own currency. Under the AOC, Congress was the only central government of the U.S., but the individual states had more authority than Congress. Under the U.S. Constitution (our second constitution), there were three separate branches of government (the tripartite government), each with different functions, but each individually equal in authority (according to the theory). Under the U.S. Constitution, the federal government could raise its own revenue (money), declare war, raise

its own military, regulate trade between states, and had supremacy over the states.

11. The Annapolis Convention: The 1786 meeting of nine state delegations in Annapolis, Maryland that demanded that the Continental Congress convene a constitutional convention to fix the Articles of Confederation.

12. The Virginia and New Jersey Plans: These were two of the most influential strategies of the constitutional convention. The Virginia Plan was the strategy for the big states, and the New Jersey Plan the perspective for the small states. The Virginia Plan asked for proportionate representation, or representation to the U.S. Senate and to the House of Representatives based on a state's population. The New Jersey Plan asked for representation based on equal votes for every state, no matter the size. The Virginia Plan also asked for a court system and a president as chief executive. The Connecticut Plan presented the great compromise between these two strategies: the U.S. Senate would be based on equal votes (every state would get two Senators) and the House would be based on population—the bigger states got more votes in that part of Congress. There would also be a chief executive or president (like a CEO of a large company) and a national court.

13. Forms of Majority Rule: There are four forms of majority rule (also called Popular Consent or Popular Sovereignty) in American government: Simple Majority (50 percent + 1), Two Thirds Majority (66 percent), Three Fourths Majority (75 percent, and Consensus (100 percent). There is also Plurality, which acts like a majority, but is not. It just means whoever gets the most votes, wins, whether it is a majority of the votes cast or not.

14. Standard Forms of Government: Monarchy (inherited rulership), Theocracy (church and state rulership under a religious authority), Oligarchy (rulership by a small committee), Autocracy (one person rulership), and Democracy (government determined by the governed).

15. Forms of Democracy: Republican (process of electing representatives to handle one's interests; also caused proxy democracy), Parliamentary (sole political authority in the hands of an elected legislature), Constitutional (a written document that contains the fundamental rules for having one's interests satisfied in a democratic government), Direct (having the constituency take care of its own interests without

sending a representative to do it), and Indirect (the broadest form, which allows representatives to be elected, selected, or appointed).

16. Political Constituency: The people or community who are governed and who participate in deciding how they will be governed.

17. Interest Groups and Political Compromise: Individuals who join together to seek benefits or political advantage based on a common agreement. Political compromises are the resolution of impasses or stalemates so that every group or participant gets part of the benefits they seek, but none gets all. A compromise is what happens when absolute and comparative advantages don't work.

18. Bicameralism: A two-house or two-chamber legislature. The legislature is a law-making body. The federal legislature is Congress, and it is divided into the House of Representatives and the U.S. Senate. Every state in the union (except Nebraska) has a bicameral legislature. In California, ours is called the State Assembly and the State Senate.

19. Inherent Powers and Delegated Powers: Inherent powers are those a country gets simply by being a country, including the right to trade with other countries and the right to make treaties and have ambassadors between countries. Delegated (or Enumerated) powers are those that are specified for each branch of government by the U.S. Constitution. For example, the president alone is the commander-in-chief of the military, only Congress can pass legislation, and only the Court can declare a law unconstitutional. The delegated powers are in articles I, II, and III of the U.S. Constitution.

20. Proportionate and Equal Representation: See #12.

21. Popular Consent and Popular Sovereignty (aka, Majority Rule): See #13.

22. Partisan Politics: Voting only the party line, that is, if you are a Republican, you vote only or the Republican agenda, or when you are a Democrat, you vote only for the Democratic agenda.

23. Five Principles of American Government: Majority Rule, The Rule of Law (Constitutionalism), Republicanism (Elected Representatives), Judicial Review (Court Review of all laws to comply with the Constitution), and Political Compromise.

24. Colonies and Colonial Governments: See pp. 11, 35–36.

25. Electoral College: The U.S. Congress meeting in Washington, D.C. for every presidential election (every four years) to count the electoral

votes cast by every state (the combination of equal representation and population). Each state's electoral vote is based on that combination. Thus California, the state with the largest population, has fifty-five electoral votes (two U.S. Senators and fifty-three Representatives to the U.S. House), while Rhode Island, one of the smallest, has only five (two U.S. Senators and three Representatives to the U.S. House).

26. General and Express Powers: The powers of the federal government as identified in Article I, Section 8 of the U.S. Constitution (for example, the power to raise revenue, thus the IRS, and the power to print money, thus the Benjamins, Jeffersons, and Jacksons).

27. Specific/Enumerated Powers: Please see #19.

28. Concurrent Powers: Authority given by the U.S. Constitution to the federal government and to the states. Examples include the power to collect income tax, to operate education systems, to have police forces, to operate welfare and healthcare systems (Medicare and Medicaid), etc.

29. Reserve Powers: Authority not expressly given to the federal government and not prohibited to the states is to stay in the hands of the states. This is the 10th Amendment, or the States' Rights Amendment. For example, the federal government cannot dictate to a state what kind of flag it can fly, or the kind of state song or state bird it can have. So the rebel flag still flies all over the South.

30. Charters: These were private property deeds given to each colony in America as a legal basis for each colony's existence. Some charters or deeds allowed for future expansion and growth, while others did not. So Virginia, Massachusetts, North Carolina and Georgia had the property deeds to expand all the way out to Nevada, Utah, and California. Delaware, New Jersey, Maryland, etc., which were small, did not have the legal authority to get any bigger. In order to get the AOC passed as America's first Constitution, the small states used their leverage (all states had to agree or the AOC became null and void) to demand that the big states give up their charter rights to expand, or the small states would not ratify the AOC.

31. Tripartite Government: The three branches of the U.S. government: the Congress, the president, the judiciary.

32. Checks and Balances: Each branch has the power and authority to nullify the authority of the other two branches. Thus, Congress can

pass legislation, the president can sign it or veto it, and the Court can review it and declare it unconstitutional, thus killing it.

33. Confederation/Federation/Unitary: The three principal ways that national governments all over the world are organized. All national governments have central authorities and all have districts, states, satellites, or regional components. Confederation means the central authority is weak and the regional or state components maintain most of the governmental authority (also called statism). Federation means the central government is organized into a partnership with its regional or state components so that each shares the authority. Unitary organization means that the central authority retains sole authority to create and dissolve district and regional branches of government.

34. Governor's Cabinet: An appointed group during the colonial era whose primary interest was making money for its members and/or for the crown, and ensuring that its members maintained the privileges of money and property. This group is the second half of the bicameral legislative body during America's colonial period and was the forerunner to the U.S. Senate (comparable to the British House of Lords).

35. Political Leverage: Having control of resources that those who want power must come to you to get. Examples include voting numbers, huge amounts of money, and authority over Congressional committees.

36. Political Ideology: A deep-seated belief in how to change or maintain the status quo (the present arrangement of things). The most basic political ideologies are conservative (not changing the status quo, keeping it the way it is), and liberal (trying to change the status quo by working within the system to expand it or create new opportunities; for example, more jobs for minorities without changing the structure of the job market).

37. Five Basic Principles of American Government: Majority Rule (Popular Consent, aka Popular Sovereignty), Constitutionalism, Republicanism, Citizen Rights, and Checks and Balances.

38. Preferred Freedoms Test: One of the federal court's (usually invented by the Supreme Court) evaluations (or doctrines) used to measure whether the government will be allowed to violate citizen rights. The Preferred Freedoms are generally recognized as freedom of speech, religion and the press (although the Courts have frequently vacillated over the latter).

39. Wall of Separation: One of the basic ingredients of American law, the separation of religion (church) and government (state), based on the 1st Amendment's prohibition that "Congress shall not establish any religion."

40. Bad Tendency Doctrine: Another one of the federal court's standard evaluations (tests) to determine whether the government will be allowed to violate citizen rights. In this case, the BTD refers to speech or writing that can be prohibited by government if the government can demonstrate that such speech or writing threatens to overthrow the government or otherwise to injure/damage the public welfare. It was first used in the *Gitlow* case.

41. Clear and Present Danger Test: An early doctrine used by the federal court to determine when the circumstances within which speech was used created an obvious threat to public safety, as in falsely yelling "fire" in a crowded room to cause panic.

42. Civil Rights: Individual rights of American citizens guaranteed in law, including original constitutional protections (especially the 14th Amendment) and Congressional legislation not deemed unconstitutional (e.g., VRA, CRA).

43. Civil Liberties: The legal rights of all members of American society (both citizens and non-citizens) protected by the first ten amendments (Bill of Rights) to the U.S. Constitution, usually also including the 14th Amendment.

44. Full Faith and Credit Clause: Part of Article IV of the Constitution in which each of the states of the country is mandated to give full legal credence to the laws and regulations of the other states (e.g., a legal deed for property recognized in one state is to also be recognized in all states).

45. Privileges and Immunities Clause: Also part of Article IV in which each of the states of the U.S.A. is mandated to provide to the citizens of the U.S.A. all of the available privileges and protections that citizens in general have (police protection, etc.).

46. Extradition, Rendition, Sedition: States have a constitutional mandate to surrender or give up fugitives into their midst who have run from criminal charges in other states; states and territories were to "render" or send back fugitive slaves when demanded from other states; and

edition is essentially treason against the U.S.A. (often defined as words or deeds in rebellion against the government).

Seventeenth Amendment: Changed the election of U.S. Senators from state legislatures to a direct vote from the general population.

. Nineteenth Amendment: 1920, gave women the right to vote (and thereby to run for office) in American elections.

49. Police Powers and Entitlements: Police power, possessed by most levels of American government, is the inherent power to impose restrictions on the private rights of citizens in order to protect the greater good of public welfare, security, and public order. Entitlements represent another name for legal rights and claims established by government for citizens and residents (e.g., once legally declared eligible to receive monthly welfare funds, a citizen can sue the government if those funds are henceforth delayed or frozen while the citizen is still eligible).

50. Intergovernmental Relations: A standard term to describe both formal (legal) and informal cooperation between two or more branches of government. For example, for FEMA to operate properly in disaster relief there must be a strategic plan of action—identifying who is responsible for what—between the federal, state, and local governments. In terms of terrorist and criminal threats, the FBI, CIA, and other law enforcement agencies are supposed to cooperate and share information.

51. Examples of Writs: Writ of Mandamus (public officials can be held accountable to do their jobs); writ of habeas corpus ("show the body," meaning accused persons must be either charged within a certain time or released from arrest); and writ of certiorari (the process by which cases are appealed to the U.S. Supreme Court). A writ simply means a law or legal proceeding.

52. Examples of Clauses: See #45 and #46. Also, the "Free Exercise Clause" (Congress shall allow the "free exercise of religion"—1st Amendment); the Establishment Clause (Congress shall not establish any religion—1st Amendment); the Elastic Clause, aka the Necessary and Proper Clause (Congress may make all laws that it deems "necessary and proper" for the nation to function—Article I); Due Process Clause (citizens shall not be deprived of life, liberty, or property without "due process" of the law—5th and 14th Amendments).

53. Interstate Compacts: A type of Intergovernmental Relations in which states formally agree to be jointly responsible for activities (e.g., interstate highways).

54. Prior Restraint: Another federal court evaluation procedure (Supreme Court Doctrine) concerning whether the government can prohibit speech or publication before it actually occurs based on what negative effect the government thinks will occur if the speech or public writing is allowed. Used a lot early on but is now very rarely used by the courts because of the Preferred Freedoms Doctrine and other factors.

55. Original Jurisdiction of the Supreme Court: Cases that start (and end) in the Supreme Court, such as country-to-country suits, state-to-state suits, etc. See Article III.

56. Thirteenth, Fourteenth, and Fifteenth Amendments: The Civil War amendments that legally ended slavery, except when incarcerated (13th), made African Americans citizens (14th), and gave them the right to vote (15th).

57. Exclusionary Rule: Police are restricted from prosecuting citizens and residents on evidence secured without a search warrant, or in compliance with other court rules (e.g., probable cause, open containers in plain sight, etc.). This rule is derived from the *Mapp v. Ohio* case.

58. *Gitlow v. New York*: The 1925 case that represented the court's first major use of the BTD discussed in #41 as a basis to allow the prior restraint of publication.

59. *Lemon v. Kurtzman*: The 1971 case which established restrictions on giving public tax money to Catholic schools and called it a violation of the "Wall of Separation."

60. Dual, Cooperative, and Regulatory Federalism: Types or styles of federal organization of the partnership with states. Dual (or layer cake) is the first dominant form used in the U.S.A. and mandated that the central government had its specific and distinct authority (nation-to-nation relations, international trade and treaties, etc.) and states retained their own individual authority (elections, state flags, etc.) and one should not interfere with the other. Cooperative federalism (aka marble cake) viewed all levels of government in the U.S.A. as part of one single government and thus they were all intertwined with each other, ensuring mutual interference. Regulatory federalism is the relationship between all branches of government based almost exclusively

on the legal requirements or regulations for each level of government's responsibility. Unfortunately, this allows each branch to claim, "it's not my problem or responsibility, it's yours."

61. *Gibbons v. Ogden*: Essentially, one of the first major uses of the supremacy clause to settle a dispute between the federal and state governments.

62. Forms of Central Government: Control of Federalism, includes Grants-in-Aid (Categorical Grants), General Purpose Grants, Block Grants (Money); Unfunded Mandates (federal order to the states to complete some public project but without providing the state any money to do so); and Preemption (federal seizure of state authority even when the state seems to be capable of handling such authority).

Credits

1. "Preamble for the Free African Society." Copyright in the Public Domain.
2. "Articles of Incorporation for the Free African Society." Copyright in the Public Domain.
3. "The Articles of Confederation." Copyright in the Public Domain.
4. "The Constitution for the United States of America." Copyright in the Public Domain.

CPSIA information can be obtained
at www.ICGtesting.com
Printed in the USA
FSOW03n0558300817
38141FS